Feather, Norman.
    Lord Rutherford.

Lord Rutherford

W.R.
1925

Rutherford, 1925
From the portrait drawing by Sir William Rothenstein
(Reproduced by kind permission of the artist)

Lord Rutherford

Norman Feather PhD, FRS

Professor of Natural Philosophy
in the University of Edinburgh

Foreword by
Professor Sir Harrie Massey FRS
Department of Physics and Astronomy
University College, London

PRIORY PRESS LIMITED

SBN 85078 157 4
Copyright © 1940 by Norman Feather

First published in 1940 by
Blackie & Son, Ltd., Glasgow
This new edition published in 1973
by Priory Press Limited
101 Grays Inn Road, London WC1

Printed photolitho in Great Britain by
J. W. Arrowsmith, Winterstoke Road, Bristol

Foreword

A WHOLE new era of science, and particularly nuclear science, has passed since the first publication of this book thirty-two years ago. The large scale application of nuclear energy and the extraordinary development of experimental techniques for exploring even more deeply the inner structure of matter, the giant accelerators, bubble chambers and spark chambers of the present day, are beyond the range of even Rutherford's vision. He would equally have been amazed and without doubt fascinated, with the discoveries made of the strange particles though perhaps a little disappointed with the apparent complexity of things at the subnuclear level.

Nevertheless, Rutherford remains the father of it all, in many ways the very epitome of the ideal scientist we would all like to be. The qualities which made him so successful remain the vital qualities today—his enthusiasm, his intuitive understanding, his humanity, his ability to inspire, his capacity for leadership, his flair for selecting the important experiments to perform, would still have led him to an outstanding position in scientific research in fundamental physics today.

All of us who had the privilege of working with him at the Cavendish Laboratory remember him not only with the greatest admiration but also with the greatest affection.

It is most important that, in these times when nuclear science is 'big' science in which teams of research workers use very large and costly equipment and when there is much questioning of scientific values and aims, that an account of the life of a truly great scientist of the comparatively recent past, written by one who knew and worked with him, should be available to the new generation of scientists who have grown up since his death. Professor Feather's book is such an account and it if most timely that the new edition should be available just after the centenary of Rutherford's birth. The fact that it was written at a time when the great scientific events of the thirties were still very fresh gives it an added value. It conveys much of the exciting atmosphere of the times as well as explaining the way in which the science unfolded.

H. S. W. Massey

20th December, 1972.

Preface

There were many sides to Rutherford's character little
suspected by those who knew him only slightly, or were
familiar merely with his large output of scientific work.
Yet one of these less known characteristics has enormously facilitated the task of his biographers: it appears
that Rutherford very rarely destroyed any document,
however trivial its contents. From his early days as a
research student, to his last years as Cavendish Professor,
a great bulk of material has been carefully preserved:
almost the whole of his personal correspondence, it
must be presumed, and all his notebooks and papers.
But for the existence of this material I should not have
known Rutherford, at first hand, earlier than the last
dozen years of his life; had not most of it already been
thoroughly sifted for the official biography,* when it
came to me, it would undoubtedly have taken me much
longer than it did, to extend my knowledge of him,
systematically, as I was able to do. I wish to thank
Professor A. S. Eve most cordially for agreeing that I
might reap the benefit of his labours in this way, and,
in this connexion, to thank Lady Rutherford, also, for
extending to me the permission which ensured access
to the letters.

Whenever possible I have attempted to obtain the
consent of the original writers to the inclusion of extracts
from letters which Rutherford received; I trust that

* Cambridge University Press, 1939.

vii

from those whom I have not been able to reach I may count on the same goodwill as I have uniformly received from those who have answered my requests. Lastly, I am fortunate in having been able to submit the whole book, in proof, to Professor J. Chadwick's criticism, and I am glad to acknowledge the help which his various remarks conveyed. In the matter of the illustrations, I owe a debt of gratitude to Sir William Rothenstein for allowing me to use as frontispiece a reproduction of his portrait drawing of Lord Rutherford, and I must not forget to thank Mr. R. Aves, of the Cavendish Laboratory, for the care with which he prepared the prints for all the plates.

To readers of this book I would point out that the emphasis all through is on Rutherford the Scientist, and that a short introductory chapter (pp. 1–16) seemed to me a necessary preliminary, if his achievements as Scientist were to be seen in true perspective, by anyone who was not already something of a specialist in these matters himself. On this last point, however, my readers may well disagree with me.

NORMAN FEATHER.

24th October, 1939.

Contents

List of Illustrations

CHAPTER I

The Outlook of the Scientist

IT is one of the easy generalizations which express half truths, to classify great men as men of action or men of thought. In so far as this classification is valid, it must always be more difficult to communicate the essence of greatness when the subject of that greatness belongs to the latter class. Men of action change frontiers; men of thought modify ideas. Then, only when the original ideas form part of a broad outlook upon the world, can the significance of any modification be properly assessed. Evidently, if this were the whole story in respect of the great men of science, every attempt to exhibit their greatness to the general public would unquestionably fail. It would lack the interest necessary to sustain it, for the ideas of the scientist have no wide currency in the world at large. In respect of men of science, however, often enough this is the beginning, not the end, of the story; ultimately a revolution in common practice follows the academic modification of ideas, and a new accession of power becomes available for human society. Such technological progress has been a marked feature of the social history of recent times. On this account, therefore, popular interest is assured, but the greatness of the scientist is not, thereby alone, rendered one degree less incomprehensible to the ordinary man. Generally, when some new instrument in the equipment of civilization excites wonder, it is the mystery of the instrument itself, rather than the broad sweep of the basic principles of science, upon which amazement dwells: it is with the electrical gadgeteer, for example, more often than with Maxwell or Hertz, that the marvel of radio-communication is commonly associated. Interest is assured, but it remains the task of the biographer to establish the basis upon which some real appreciation of the contribution of the man of thought—the scientist—to human achievement can popularly rest. Moreover, if this be true in respect of Maxwell, whose greatest contribution to ideas already underlies technological applications of immense importance, it is even more true for the subject of the present biography, Rutherford, father of nuclear physics, whose far-reaching contributions to the ideological structure of science have as yet no immediate bearing on any of the material adjuncts of civilization. In this instance, in particular, a popular biography of the scientist must obviously be prefaced by some attempt at a general introduction to that branch of science with which his life's work has dealt. Without this, the account will appear of trifling significance; in the light of it, it may be possible not only to attain a clear idea of the greatness of Rutherford, the scientist, but also, through the particular details which his biography provides, to consolidate that general notion of the scope and limitations of science which this introduction can do little more than briefly sketch. Indeed, there can be no better guide to an understanding of the abstract principles of the subject than to follow the development of ideas in the pioneer work of a master of experimental science. We have, then, first of all, to try to know something of the methods of the physical scientist and the limited validity of his conclusions, and, secondly, to understand the essentials of the world-picture to which he had come towards the end of the last century, when the work of Rutherford began.

In physical science we have heard much of the distinction between experimenter and theorist: it has been said [1] " The task of science is both to extend the range of our experience and to reduce it to order ". Here, it would appear, the two rôles are clearly distinguished. Yet, on further analysis, this clarity disappears and the distinction loses much of its force. The theorist is required not only after the experiment, to interpret the results, but beforehand, to suggest what experiment should be performed. Broadly speaking, experimental physics began in the time of Galileo: two thousand years before this the Greeks, in a long succession from Thales onwards, had " had the genius to be astonished " [2], passively recognizing the diversity of phenomena in nature and making theories which they imagined might account for them. With the Greeks, also, a great development in mathematics originated. It is important at the outset to contrast these two modes of thought. The classical picture of the world failed when confronted with the results of observation and experiment; the elaboration of Greek mathematics, on the other hand, ultimately suggested the type of experiment by which these decisive results were obtained. " Apart from this progress of mathematics," Whitehead says,[3] " the seventeenth century developments of science would have been impossible. Mathematics supplied the background of imaginative thought with which the men of science approached the

---

[1] Bohr, *Atomic Theory and the Description of Nature*, 1934, p. 1.
[2] Whitehead, *Adventures of Ideas*, 1933, p. 191.
[3] *Science and the Modern World*, 1925, p. 46.

observation of nature." What mathematics actually supplied was a system of ideas, logically developed, of such generality and internal consistency that on the face of things they had no direct application to nature at all. The achievement of the early experimental physicists, as it now appears, was the discovery that there are wide aspects of natural phenomena to which these ideas apply. Number, and, in geometry, certain simple types of measurement, are basic mathematical ideas; experimental physics has developed into the science of measurement on a more grandiose scale. On this view, too, the system of theory in use at any time represents the attempt to bring together, in a growing synthesis, a picture of those aspects of nature which have already proved susceptible of measurement. On the basis of this picture the extension of experiment into new domains naturally suggests itself.

If this analysis be correct, then obviously the experimenter in physics, whether he be a professional mathematician or not, in one important sense must also be regarded as a theorist; if he were to describe the reasons which prompt his experiments, or the results which he has obtained from them, he would be making use of language which is without precise meaning except within the scheme of theoretical physics in general use at the time. The words " atom ", " electron ", " nucleus ", which will recur again and again throughout this biography, along with many others, belong to this language.

Here we have expressed briefly the view of the limitations of science; the contrary opinion holds, essentially, that the methods of the physical sciences are ultimately applicable to a survey of the whole of reality. Whilst this opinion can be expressed so crudely as at once to excite suspicion, in practice it is commonly implicit in our general outlook upon affairs. There are many reasons for this result. The scientist, absorbed in his own experiments, sees no end to the particular applications of the method of science in his special field of inquiry; he approaches each problem which arises by this method and looks for its resolution, sooner or later, with complete confidence. It does not lead to efficiency that he should burden himself with the " constant remembrance of the struggle of novel thought with the obtuseness of language." [1] He writes his scientific treatises from cover to cover without ever allowing this struggle to distract the reader's attention. When he says " The atom is naturally the most fundamental structure presented to us. Its properties must explain the properties of all more complicated structures, including matter in bulk. . . ." [2] he speaks with a directness which shows that all consciousness of the use of an elaborate idiom has been lost. He may remember something of that idiom, from time to time, and recognize the severely selective nature of his experimental approach—" The rapidity and certitude of the advance in this epoch have largely depended on the fact that it has been possible to devise experiments so that few variables were involved " [3]—but his efficiency as scientist, it must be repeated, depends largely upon his forgetfulness in this respect. On the other hand, the general reader of his biography should not be equally forgetful. He, too, by inclination, may well be disposed to disregard the limitations of science. If so, the result for him—the reader—may be more disastrous. With

---

[1] Whitehead, *Adventures of Ideas*, 1933, p. 153.

[2] Rutherford, Presidential address, British Association, 1923.

[3] Rutherford, *ibid*.

the wide public of non-scientists the evidence of almost unbelievable technological progress, based upon the results of scientific research, has led to this confusing of the trend of modern physical science with the approach to ultimate omniscience.   A brief examination of the connexion between science and useful technology indicates that this situation is not entirely without a basis of reason.   The restriction which limits physical science to those features of phenomena which are susceptible of measurement is also the restriction which ensures that calculation and detailed prediction are possible regarding future events in this limited domain. The possibility of prediction inevitably brings power. Both science and technology have limited fields—and, to a large extent, the limitations are similar.   It is to the scientist, and not, for example, to the poet, that we look for the vision that the possibility of providing men with light and heat as they desire is implicit in the association of a coil of wire and a magnet.   In such a vision the gulf between the idiom of science and the common language of everyday life is momentarily bridged.   But the poet, also, must not be denied his share in the interpretation of the world.   It has been said " The scientific picture of the world is what it is because men of science combine this incompetence [to discuss questions of æsthetics and philosophy] with certain special competences." [1]   If this is accepted, it only remains for us to inquire what in fact the scientific picture of the world was at the end of the nineteenth century, in order to be in a position to follow and appreciate the changes in that picture which are to be attributed directly and indirectly to the work of Rutherford, which is our main concern.

[1] Aldous Huxley, *Ends and Means*, 1937, p. 268.

Towards the end of the nineteenth century it was generally believed by men of science that it would eventually be possible, in so far as complete success had not then been achieved, to describe the phenomena of the material universe in terms of the motions of massive particles moving under the influence of forces. This description, it was thought, would continue to employ the ideas of space and time, of mass and force, developed two hundred years previously by Newton—and it was tacitly assumed that these ideas would be found to be valid in the sub-microscopic world, the domain of minute distances and enormous velocities, as they were certainly valid for the large-scale effects in respect of which they had first been developed. The scientists of the nineteenth century were, most of them, atomists; as we have just stated, they further believed that the Newtonian mechanics provided the appropriate mathematical apparatus for describing the motions of atoms. Here it is worth while discussing the origin of the atomic hypothesis in somewhat greater detail than this—and examining Newton's own account, written in his later years, of how he arrived at the general dynamical laws with which we are concerned.

Newton wrote: " In this philosophy particular propositions are inferred from the phenomena, and afterwards rendered general by induction. Thus it was that the impenetrability, the mobility, and the impulsive force of bodies, and the laws of motion and gravitation, were discovered " [1]—and, in another place, " the arguing from experiments and observations by induction . . . is the best way of arguing which the nature of things admits of . . . if no exception occur from

[1] General Scholium, *Philosophiae Naturalis Principia Mathematica*, 2nd edition, 1713.

phenomena, the conclusions may be pronounced generally.   But if at any time afterwards any exception
shall occur from experiments, it may then begin to be
pronounced with such exceptions as occur." [1]   Although
in these passages Newton may not appear as a very
profound philosopher, at least he indicates one of the
fundamental procedures of the scientific method.   Yet,
it will be noted, the following out of this particular procedure could never by itself lead to the idea of atoms.
The method of induction describes observed regularities
in terms which have already been defined;   rigidly
adhered to it makes no provision for the definition of
new terms or the framing of " explanatory " hypotheses.
The notion of the atomic constitution of matter, after
surviving for more than two thousand years as an element in speculative philosophy, did not attain to the
rank of an explanatory hypothesis until roughly a
hundred years after the death of Newton.   As we shall
presently discover, it was the work of Rutherford, early
in the twentieth century, which advanced its status still
farther, exhibiting it as the very foundation of the
whole scheme of interpretation which is the theoretical
basis of physical science to-day.

In Newton's time the idea of atoms was commonly
held, very much as it had been inherited from the later
Greeks, as a philosophical belief: no experimental
method had been devised for estimating how many
such entities were to be thought of as present in a given
piece of matter, nor of arriving at any understanding of
the differences in form, mass, or motion which ought
to be postulated as between the atoms of one substance
and those of another.   As far as experimental physics was
concerned, Newton might well have written, regarding

[1] *Opticks*, 1704.

the idea of atoms, what in fact he wrote in another connexion, " What I am not satisfied in, I can scarce esteem fit to be communicated to others; especially in natural philosophy, where there is no end of fancying." [1] We have already indicated, however, that sounder reasons for indulging in precisely this type of fancying began to be recognized just short of a hundred years after Newton died.   In chemistry the notions of " element " and " compound " were by that time beginning to be accepted in something like their present form, about twenty different chemical elements had already been distinguished, and a large amount of quantitative work on chemical combination had been done.   On the basis of these results—and after consideration of a great deal of purely physical evidence concerning the behaviour of gases and vapours as regards compression and solution—John Dalton put forward the view that the essential distinction between one elementary substance and another was ultimately to be described in terms of the differences between the atoms of which these substances were constituted.   There were, therefore, as many different types of atom as there were chemical elements; chemical combination was the union of atoms of different elements into certain simple structures of definite types—the atoms (or, as we should now say, the " molecules ") of the compound substances so produced—and, for practical purposes most important of all, gravimetric analysis, giving the constitution by weight of a large number of chemical compounds, made possible the determination of the relative weights (masses) which had to be assigned to the atoms themselves.   Modern chemical science dates from the

---

[1] Newton to Boyle, 1676.

enunciation of this most successful of simplifying hypotheses (1803–10).

Further simplification followed when another range
of experimental results was "explained" in terms of
the new hypothesis, by the statement that the number
of molecules in unit volume is the same for all gases
compared under the same conditions of temperature
and pressure (Avogadro, 1811; Ampère, 1814). The
very simplicity of such a statement might be regarded
as good reason for confidence that the atomic picture of
the constitution of matter is fundamentally significant.
Yet, again, for nearly fifty years more, there was no
trustworthy evidence concerning the size, or the absolute
—as distinct from the relative—mass, of the atoms, and
there was a complete lack of discovered phenomena
which might be described in terms of the behaviour of
single atoms, or even of relatively small numbers of
atoms. Moreover, from an early stage, it must also
have been clear, on very little consideration, that many
of the broad differences in properties which distinguish
one elementary substance from another—for example
differences in electrical and thermal conductivity, in
magnetic and certain optical properties, differences in
hardness and in melting point—were not to be explained
simply in terms of differences in mass and size amongst
the irreducible atoms of matter. Nevertheless the atomic
hypothesis, even in its original form, was so nearly
indispensable to the chemist that its retention was
inevitable. In the early years of the second half of the
century the first successful application of this same
hypothesis to a wide range of physical phenomena led
directly to that feeling of expectation among scientists,
which has already been alluded to, that ultimately
all the phenomena of the material universe would be

described in a similar way. Between the years 1850 and 1880 nearly all the properties of matter in the gaseous state were "explained" in terms of the motion of molecules. In the dynamical theory of gases, which in very closely its original form still provides this explanation to-day, only the mass and size of the molecule—and, for certain refinements, the number of atoms which it contains—are used to distinguish one particular kind of gas from another. What had successfully been achieved for the gaseous state, it was supposed, would eventually be possible for the solid and liquid states also.

During the development of the dynamical theory of gases more exact ideas concerning the mass and size of the still hypothetical atoms were arrived at. It will clarify our thought, perhaps, to try to appreciate, at this stage, the extreme smallness of these units and to see how fine-grained the structure of matter must be supposed to be in the light of the experimental results. Suppose that we take a large-sized cabin trunk which is "empty" according to standard usage—that is full of air under ordinary conditions. Let us consider the spatial arrangement of the molecules in this volume of air at some instant. Beginning with any molecule, let us imagine a line drawn to its nearest neighbour, continued from this to the molecule nearest to it again, and so on—touching every molecule once only, until all have been accounted for. The number of molecules in such a volume of air is so great that if our zig-zag line were now to be straightened out it would reach from the earth to the nearest of the fixed stars—a distance which it takes three or four years for light to travel. A slightly greater distance would be covered if the same procedure were adopted with the molecules in a gallon of water. In a liquid like water we suppose that most of the volume is accounted for by the bulk of the molecules themselves; in the air more than 99·9 per cent of the volume is empty space, occupied but not filled by the moving molecules.

By 1890 the atomic theory of matter, as we have now seen, had become firmly established; the atomic theory of electricity, on the other hand, had at that time only recently received serious consideration. It is true that in 1881 Helmholtz had written: " If we accept the hypothesis that elementary substances are composed of atoms, we cannot avoid concluding that electricity also is divided into elementary portions which behave like atoms of electricity ", but so strong a conviction as this had previously been far from general. Even Maxwell had expressed his doubts in *A Treatise on Electricity and Magnetism* (1873)—" The theory of molecular charges may serve as a method by which we may remember a good many facts. . . . It is extremely improbable, however, that . . . we shall retain in any form the theory of molecular charges;"—and these remarks had been allowed to stand by his editors in two subsequent editions (1881 and 1892). Inasmuch as Rutherford began his advanced studies in science in the year that the third edition of Maxwell's treatise was published, and made his first contact with physics in England just at the time when the atomic theory of electricity was to receive its final justification, we shall do well to complete our review of the important notions in theoretical physics which he inherited, by further attention to the developments which led up to this hypothesis. Moreover, as regards these developments, particular interest must necessarily attach to the precise experimental facts which, as Helmholtz interpreted them, provided the logical connexion between views as to the atomicity of matter, on the one hand, and the atomicity of electric charge, on the other. The closeness of this connexion is the important question for discussion.

During the century and a half to which we may limit consideration, two distinct phases in the history of experimental electricity may be clearly distinguished. For the first fifty years (1740–90) practically all the experiments were concerned with electricity at rest; during the last hundred years (1790–1890) almost all had to do with electricity in motion. The tacit assumption which underlies this statement of the situation— that both sets of phenomena were due to a single agent " electricity ", opera. .ng in different circumstances, was established as correct by the investigations of Wollaston in 1801. Broadly speaking, however, the two series of experiments provided evidence for quite different characteristics of this fundamental agent (or substance). The early experiments in static electricity had quite unmistakably shown that two types of electrification could be produced, related to one another in quality in a manner conveniently expressed by the designations " positive " and " negative " electricity—these adjectives carrying the usual algebraic significance—yet subsequent experiments on current electricity, for a long time at least, provided no evidence of this qualitative distinction. Before the distinction reappeared, in the interpretation of such experiments, the first general theories of electricity had been put forward and had been greatly elaborated by mathematical analysis.

We may obtain some idea of the nature of these theories, at the time of their formulation, from the following statements by Benjamin Franklin, the originator of the so-called " one-fluid " theory:

" The electrical matter consists of particles extremely subtile, since it can permeate common matter, even the densest metals, with such ease and freedom as not to receive any perceptible resistance. . . .

" But though the particles of electrical matter do repel each other, they are strongly attracted by all other matter."

These statements were made in 1749. They show that at this early stage the " fluid " theories were also in a certain sense, atomic theories of electricity—although the electrical atoms may have been supposed to be so " subtile " as to be entirely devoid of mass. However, before long, the thorough-going mathematical ela- boration, which unified the various " fluid " theories, and was in full course of development at the beginning of the nineteenth century, soon removed even this trace of atomism: all questions of the structure of these hypothetical electrical fluids then became irrelevant in the final symbolization. It has been said " physicists and mathematicians . . . refined and idealized the conception of these fluids until any reference to their physical properties was considered almost indelicate." For present purposes the chief fact to be recorded is that this idealization provided a very successful mathe- matical theory of electrical effects which did not concern itself too deeply with the nature of electricity.

It was not until the passage of electricity through liquid and gaseous, as distinct from solid metallic, conductors began to be studied, that the question of the ultimate nature of electricity again received serious consideration.   During the years 1833–4 Faraday devoted much of his time to the study of the phenomena of electrolysis—the chemical decomposition of certain substances dissolved in water, which occurs when a current of electricity is passed between metal plates (electrodes) immersed in the liquid. Faraday himself described the final result of these investigations by a very simple generalization, which in present-day terminology we might express as follows: If the same constant current be passed through a number of electrolytic cells containing different substances in solution, the weights of the different products, obtained at the electrodes in a definite time, are proportional to the chemical combining weights of these products. Since, on the basis of the atomic theory of matter, we have already agreed (p. 9) that the chemical combining weights are closely related to the relative weights (masses) of the individual atoms of the elements, it appears, from Faraday's results, that the passage of a given quantity of electricity is always attended by the liberation of the same number, or a closely related number, of atoms, whatever substance be considered. We might say that with each atom, or group of atoms, in electrolysis, there must be associated a single fixed amount, or a closely related amount, of electricity—either positive or negative. A natural unit, or atom, of electricity appears thus to be indicated—and the original distinction between positive and negative electrification reappears.

Unless we remember the ideological background of the mathematical theory of electricity employed at the time, it seems very curious indeed that so simple an interpretation of these results should have to wait nearly fifty years (1834 to 1881) for widespread recognition and acceptance. To begin with, perhaps, the atomic theory of matter was not sufficiently part of the world-picture of the physicist to form a natural basis for this interpretation, but ultimately his dislike of it must, as already suggested, be attributed to the ideas which he held concerning the nature of electrification. So long as he thought in terms of an electric fluid permeating the interstices between the atoms or molecules of matter, he could not easily imagine how the material molecules themselves should become charged with electricity, let alone with an amount of electricity which was constant, under varying conditions and with different elements. In the last analysis, this was the real cause of Maxwell's objection. " The electrification of a molecule," he wrote, " though easily spoken of, is not so easily conceived." As we follow the contributions of Rutherford to physical theory throughout the remainder of this biography, we shall inevitably conclude that in this particular, at least, Helmholtz was the prophet of the new age, Maxwell the apologist of the old.

Chapter 2

Rutherford's Early Life in New Zealand

WHEN Ernest Rutherford was born, on 30th August, 1871, at Brightwater, thirteen miles south of Nelson, New Zealand, many of the first British colonists were still alive. In a fertile country, twice as big as England, there was not, even then, more than a quarter of a million white people, only fifteen years of parliamentary government had been enjoyed, and sporadic warfare with the Maoris had scarcely subsided. Already, a brief period of early prosperity had been followed by economic depression. Ernest Rutherford was born at this time, second son and fourth child in a family of twelve. His father was James Rutherford, the son of a Scots colonist who had left Dundee with his family—James Rutherford then being three years old— as one of the early settlers. His mother was an English-woman from Sussex; at the age of thirteen she had emigrated with her mother to New Zealand. His people were farmers. At Brightwater James Rutherford had a flax farm and mills, and, as was general in New Zealand at that time, employed water power almost exclusively for driving the machinery. Brightwater is situated in a well-wooded valley with distant hills on either side, and in this pleasant country, following the normal pursuits of a healthy child, Ernest Rutherford grew up. When he was six years old, legislation providing for the compulsory education of children between the ages of seven and thirteen years was introduced. It is probable that, as the result of this enactment, the future Nobel prizeman was amongst the first batch of pupils brought together " under compulsion " at the state primary school in his district—though it is strange to speak of compelling Rutherford in the search after knowledge!

There is an interesting side-light on this early period in a letter written near the end of his life, to a sister, Mrs. Strieff.   Rutherford wrote,[1] " I have recently found that I have a Savings Bank account in Nelson, N.Z., and when I was nine years old, deposited £1, 5s. 0d. in it.   This has been untouched and has now mounted up to £6, 4s. 6d.   I have an idea that I must have earned this prodigious sum of money (at that time) by helping my uncle Thomson on the farm!"   It is reported that, on another occasion, during a long summer holiday, he and his three brothers earned £13 in six weeks picking hops.   This was at Foxhill, nearly ten miles beyond Brightwater, up the valley—and at that time Rutherford was attending the public school at Havelock, a small town some distance to the east of Nelson, on the coast.   From this school at Havelock, Ernest Rutherford entered Nelson College with a scholarship from the Board of Education in 1887, at the age of fifteen, and about the same time his parents moved to Pungarehu, a township in Egmont county, Taranaki province, twenty-six miles south-west of New Plymouth.   According to the directory, even nowadays the only connexion between Pungarehu and New Plymouth is by a daily motor-bus.   At Pungarehu James Rutherford continued as a flax farmer.

This change, which took the Rutherfords from the

[1] 24th May, 1935.

South Island to the North Island of New Zealand, brought with it a marked change in natural surroundings. The broad valley at the head of Tasman Bay in which Brightwater is situated was replaced by the narrow littoral surrounding Mount Egmont, an isolated snow-clad peak, rising, in twenty miles, more than eight thousand feet out of the ocean, on three sides, with the mainland to the east of it. Multitudes of rapid streams flow through densely wooded slopes almost directly to the coast. On this littoral Pungarehu is situated, due west of the mountain and two miles from the Pacific. It is in the centre of " the garden of New Zealand ". Here Ernest Rutherford returned in vacation—to shoot pheasant and wild pigeon, to fence with his brothers, to make his own cameras and, as a keen amateur, to take photographs with them, to help on the farm or as tutor to his young sisters—and, at times, to study. It was a more vigorous life, and closer to the soil, than most English students of that age would commonly lead.

At Nelson College two members of the staff had a particular influence on the young Rutherford's education: the headmaster, W. J. Ford, who had previously been a classical master at Marlborough, and was a noted cricketer, and Dr. W. S. Littlejohn. Ford realized sufficiently the latent talent in the new scholar to place him in the fifth form when he entered the college, and Littlejohn was his teacher in mathematics and science. Rutherford's scholastic success was immediate and general. In his first year he obtained a prize for reading, and a scholarship for proficiency in history; when the year came to an end his entry into the sixth form was a matter of course. He was two years in the sixth form. At the end of the first year he was awarded scholarships for English literature and French, and carried off the form prizes in both classics and mathematics; in the second year he repeated his success in mathematics and took further prizes in English literature and Latin. During this year he gained a junior scholarship offered by the university of New Zealand, and at the end of it entered Canterbury College, Christchurch, as an undergraduate. Rutherford was placed fourth in the list of ten junior scholars elected in his year; his was the sixth success gained in this competition by students of Nelson College during the period of fourteen years for which the scheme had been working. A choice of five out of eight subjects—some carrying more and some less marks in the examination—was allowed to the candidates. Rutherford took mathematics and Latin (each carrying 1500 marks, the maximum available), English and science (with 1000 marks each), and French (with 750). In science he took the two papers in sound and light, and mechanics, rather than those in heat or magnetism and electricity. It is not difficult to see that at this stage Rutherford had a good grounding in mathematics, but very little knowledge of physics, as distinct from applied mathematics. We see, too, that the university evidently did not expect any of its scholars, on entry, to have covered, even in the most elementary fashion, more than half the subject of physics as then known. All that Rutherford knew of physics when he entered the university he may fairly be said to have learnt in private tuition from Dr. Littlejohn. Of these two, pupil and teacher, it is reported on the best authority that they spent much time on half-holidays, walking up and down the quiet streets which surrounded the college, deep in discussion of problems in mathematics and the rudiments of science. If all the details of the report be believed, the dry soil of the streets of Nelson was frequently marked out with geometrical figures and scientific designs, even as the sandy floor of Archimedes' villa in Syracuse had been, more than two thousand years previously. From the pupil who studied these designs there was soon to develop another philosopher no less famous than Archimedes himself.

Outside the classroom and his studies Ernest Rutherford took a full part in the activities of his schoolmates. He played forward at rugby football, and in his last year obtained his place in the first fifteen. He was good at single-stick; he played cricket, but at this he was not distinguished. He was elected college librarian —and filled the office with a genial despotism which was to remain with him a permanent attitude of mind in certain of his dealings with his fellow men. But he made no serious enemies thereby. Since, as a boy, he had always been a great reader, with wide interests, his choice as librarian must have been in every way a happy one. He left Nelson College for Christchurch clearly the proud product of his school. After forty years, when considerable reconstruction was made necessary through damage caused in an earthquake, one of the new boarding houses at Nelson College was named Rutherford House.

A few months before Rutherford left Nelson, Lord Onslow succeeded Sir W. D. Jervois as Governor of New Zealand. When he arrived, an address of welcome was prepared at the school and it fell to Rutherford, as head boy, to read it. His reactions to this situation were remembered by a correspondent nearly fifty years later. In February, 1937, F. J. Mules wrote to him, " I sometimes recall your reluctance to discharge your responsibilities as Head Boy and resign the duty of reading

3

Joynt's [1] address of welcome to the Governor, Lord Onslow." Obviously, then, there was a strong strain of modesty in his make-up, also.

When Canterbury College reassembled early in 1890 at least five of the year's ten junior university scholars were entered on its books. Two of the three who stood above Rutherford on the list were amongst them— W. S. Marris [2] and E. S. Buchanan. Neither of these two, however, intended to specialize in mathematics or physics. Marris, who had headed the scholarship list, though he was two years younger than Rutherford, went on to do Latin and Greek; Buchanan did modern languages. From the beginning, therefore, Rutherford was the pupil of his year in his own subject. But it must be remembered that six terms had to elapse before he was able to specialize in that subject. According to the university regulations of the time, every honours student had first to take the pass degree, which, in Arts, involved Latin and pure mathematics as compulsory subjects, and four other subjects, of which only two might be scientific. The non-scientific part of the course could not possibly be completed before the end of the second year. So it was, then, that early in 1892 Ernest Rutherford began to devote his time seriously to some advanced physics, in addition to his mathematics. In November of that year he took the last of his papers for the B.A. pass degree and sat for the university senior scholarship.

Senior scholarships were awarded for one year to enable students to complete the course for honours, and

---

[1] J. W. Joynt succeeded Ford as headmaster whilst Rutherford was a pupil at Nelson College. The Governor of New Zealand was also Visitor of the College.

[2] Later, Sir William Marris, Governor of Assam and the United Provinces.

in 1892 nine scholarships were available, one each ear-marked for the nine principal subjects of study. Actually, only eight scholarships were awarded—and five of these went to Canterbury College. Marris got the Latin scholarship, Buchanan the scholarship for English and French, and Rutherford the mathematics award. The scholarship for physical science went to J. Chisholm of Otago. Even after he had been three years at the ← university, there can be no doubt that the future Faraday was much more a mathematician than an experimental scientist.

During his honours year Rutherford took mathe-matics, and both mathematical and experimental physics. His teachers were C. H. H. Cook, professor of mathe-matics and natural philosophy, a Cambridge mathe-matician who had for a time been fellow of St. John's College, and A. W. Bickerton, who occupied the chair of chemistry and physics. Bickerton had been trained at South Kensington, at the Royal School of Mines, and was a fellow of the Chemical Society. Everyone with any direct experience of the teaching of these two men testifies to the complete dissimilarity of their methods and outlook. " Cook, thoroughly orthodox in all his views and strictly scholastic in his methods, within his limitations a very able man. . . . Bickerton, heterodox . . . very erratic in his methods of teaching, but at the same time highly original." [1] This is one attempt at comparison from one who knew them.

It is interesting to try to assess the amount and nature of the assistance which Rutherford derived from his two professors during his years of development. In the first place, in mathematics he must certainly have

[1] Rutherford obituary notice, *Proceedings of the Physical Society*, May, 1938.

owed much to the careful teaching of Cook—and here it must not be forgotten that the mathematical aspects of physics, as well as pure mathematics, formed part of that teaching—but the influence of Bickerton is more difficult to evaluate. Bickerton was nothing of a mathematician, otherwise, perhaps, his physical ideas could not have been so heterodox, but also his originality was enhanced by his completely direct approach to the problems in which he was interested. How varied these problems were may be gauged from a list of a few of the papers which he read before the Philosophical Institute of Canterbury, the local branch of the staid and very respectable New Zealand Institute (now the Royal Society of New Zealand). On the occasion when Rutherford was elected a member of the institute on 6th July, 1892, in his third year as an undergraduate, Professor Bickerton was in the chair. He was also responsible for the only communications to the society, the first " On hail " and the second " On the equilibrium of gaseous cosmic spheres ". Again, at the annual meeting on 7th November, 1894, when Rutherford himself read his first paper to the members of the institute (we shall return to the contents of this very considerable communication shortly), Professor Bickerton had seven papers standing in his name—amongst them dissertations " On molecular attraction " and " On chlorine as a cure for consumption ". There was, it seems, a strange mixture of the true scientist and the completely uninformed amateur in this remarkable individual, but, as far as his influence on Rutherford is concerned, two things at least may be said to his credit. He had boundless enthusiasm for research—and, in his more solid achievements, he showed, by his very neglect of mathematical analysis, that the experimenter does well who keeps mathematics, not as mistress, but as handmaid—and even then dispenses with her services at times.

We have already mentioned the Philosophical Institute of Canterbury, the official science society connected with the university. It is rather remarkable that, in the three years during which he was a member of the institute, Rutherford did not fill any of its offices, nor was he elected to its council. He took a slightly more active part in an unofficial College Science Society which was founded in 1891. This society was distinctly radical in its outlook and, one might imagine, rather unrestrained in its speculations. Rutherford was one of its original members, and W. G. Pye, his senior by one year, its moving spirit. Eighteen months after the society was formed, Pye took second-class honours in Latin and English. In these days of specialization it is strange to think of undergraduates, normally busy with quite elementary studies in languages and the classics, organizing, in their spare time, pretentious discussions on the broad topic of evolution—and, even if they chose to do so, neglecting, in the beginning, the more familiar biological aspect of the matter and opening with a paper on the evolution of the elements. But this was what happened in Christchurch—and the society flourished, at least during the whole period of Rutherford's connexion with the college. In 1893 he took office as secretary of the society, and in the following year read a paper, on electrical waves and oscillations, which was illustrated by several experiments. By that time, of course, Rutherford was already engaged in research, but there are points in connexion with his paper which are worthy of interest. In the first place the early history of the society had shocked the more susceptible members of the academic community; the irresponsible discussion, even the open discussion, of evolutionary doctrines, and the free speculation thereby engendered, was not regarded as profitable occupation for undergraduates.   It is recorded that Rutherford, too, felt some embarrassment on this score: he had to be tactfully handled before he would accept the secretaryship.   However, during his year of office he did his best to redeem the society from the stigma of unre-strained speculation.   Concerning his communication to the members there is a bald phrase in the society's minutes " illustrated by experiments performed by Mr. Rutherford with the assistance of Mr. Page and Mr. Erskine. . . ." [1] Here, surely, is the first flowering of Rutherford's ability as an organiser of research. Page was demonstrator in physics and chemistry and assistant to Professor Bickerton, Erskine was a promising honours student, one year junior to Rutherford, who eventually followed closely in his footsteps, obtaining first classes, and an 1851 Exhibition scholarship for electricity, just as Rutherford did.   These two, Page and Erskine, were probably the only two persons capable of rendering real assistance in the experiments: in spite of their dissimilarities, both of them were enlisted to help—and the experimental demonstration was a great success.   No one, particularly no young man, can claim assistance in this way consistently unless he possesses the charm of effortless leadership to a marked degree. That, even so early in life, Rutherford must have pos-sessed this charm, is evident from a statement of Pro-fessor Bickerton in the following year.   Bickerton wrote,[2] " Personally Mr. Rutherford is . . . so willing to help

[1] Obituary notice, *Proc. Phys. Soc.*, May, 1938.

[2] 8th May, 1895.

other students over their difficulties, that he has en-
deared himself to all who have been brought in contact
with him." No further explanation is needed.

Rutherford took his honours examination in the
November of 1893—and obtained the only first class
in mathematics or physics in the whole university.
As we have already indicated, he was a candidate in
both these subjects: he obtained first-class honours in
each of them. A double success such as this had not
been achieved, except once previously, in the history of
the university—and, on that occasion (1887) also, by
a former pupil of Dr. Littlejohn, who had preceded
Rutherford to Canterbury College. Having obtained
the highest possible honours, therefore, Rutherford
began his research. Yet it is highly improbable that, in
his own mind, he was conscious of any abrupt change
in his way of life at this time. On the one hand, he
still had, according to the traditions of the science
school of the college, some elementary examinations
to take, and, on the other, the immediate problems on
which he first researched were merely natural exten-
sions of experiments in which he had been specially
interested during his practical work for the honours
degree. We may take these two points in turn. As
regards the first point, it seems to have been the tradition
of the department that anyone remaining in the department longer than was necessary to obtain honours in
Arts (and so the degree of M.A.) should proceed to
qualify for the pass degree in science (B.Sc.). In Rutherford's case this involved elementary work in biology
and botany, and probably also in chemistry, during his
fifth year at the college. There is still extant a stiff-
backed notebook in which he began to take notes of
lectures in these subjects. At one end of the book are

the notes on botany; starting from the other end those
on biology. Obviously, these two sets of notes are the
work of one who was not completely absorbed in the
subject of the moment; in the margins are monograms
and geometrical designs—and in one place occurs the
memorandum " what does a gown and hood cost?"
The two sets of notes never met in the middle of the
book. In biology the end comes with the remark " Liv-
ing bodies do not obey solely the law of Physics "—
and, as if to emphasize that this was indeed a fitting
point at which to drop the whole matter, the very next
page contains " Particulars of a steel wire ring " which
had been used in some physical experiments! Almost
in the middle of this notebook a passage of extreme
interest illustrates, better than anything else could
possibly do, the second point which was mentioned
above. Under the date 5th December, 1893—and this
is practically the only date in the whole notebook—
there is a description of " Experiments on secondary
circuits ". According to the syllabus of the honours
course, Rutherford must certainly have carried out
class experiments on this subject during the previous
year, and doubtless, being the most advanced experiments in that course, they interested him particularly.
But it is hardly an average first-class honours student,
who, less than a month after his examination, finds the
energy to return to a class problem, however interesting
it may have been, or to write an introduction to his
embryonic researches at once so restrained and so confident as the passage which follows:

" After reading Lord Kelvin's article on ' An
accidental illustration of the shallowness of transient
current in an iron bar ', page 473, vol. III of his

collected works and Lord Rayleigh's article in the *Philosophical Magazine* for 1886, on 'Resistance of conductors conveying alternating currents' it occurred to me that Faraday's statement of the absolute equality of the time integral of the induced current on making and breaking the circuit that this was only true in the case of very fine wires and that the thickness of the wire in the secondary circuit would have the effect of making the current at make and break different since the resistance of conductors increases with the shortness of duration of a transient current. It was not observed till later that the same idea had occurred to Sir W. Thomson in a paper in *Philosop. Magaz.* for March, 1890, entitled 'On the time integral of a transient electromagnetically induced current'."

This is the record of a mind which was already moving abreast of the development of thought in science, and was soon to lead it. In view of its great interest, the passage in question has been reproduced in facsimile on the plate facing page 27.

Maxwell, it is said, remarked on one occasion to Arthur Schuster, "I never try to dissuade a man from trying an experiment; if he does not find out what he is looking for he may find something else." [1] This is precisely what happened with Rutherford in these first researches. He did not find the difference which he had anticipated—"Faraday's result we now know is absolutely true theoretically," he remarks — but, in trying to find it, he had, for a reason which will presently appear, made the wise choice of iron wires, and he became very interested indeed in the magnetic properties of iron under various conditions. In this

[1] Maxwell Commemoration Volume, 1931, p. 22.

way he was provided with a line of work which not only lasted for the remainder of his time in New Zealand, but also occupied his attention during the early part of his scholarship at Cambridge.

The problem which Rutherford originally set himself, in the passage which has been quoted, had to do with the way in which an electric current, which is rapidly increasing or decreasing in strength, is distributed in passing through a conductor. The theoretical work which he had read suggested that, if the conductor was made of a strongly magnetic material, peculiar effects would be found. So Rutherford chose iron for his experiments, as the most strongly magnetic material available. Then, on reflection, it probably occurred to him to wonder whether, under rapidly varying magnetizing forces, iron really was as strongly magnetic as was supposed. On reading the literature he discovered accounts of other experiments which appeared to strengthen his doubts. He set to work on his investigations.

Now, if Rutherford had possessed the resources of a modern laboratory in carrying these investigations to the conclusion which he reached, it would have been a solid achievement, but we must remember that they were carried out in a cellar, which was normally used as a cloakroom by the students. The first results were published in the *Transactions of the New Zealand Institute* in 1894 under the title " Magnetization of iron by high-frequency discharges ", and a second paper on " Magnetic Viscosity " followed in the same journal in 1895. Taken together, these two papers, occupying some fifty-five pages of print, constituted at that time by far the most substantial contribution to physical research which had appeared in the *New Zealand Transactions* during the whole history of the publication—already a period of nearly thirty years. Against the prejudice of his original suspicion, Rutherford concluded, " iron is strongly magnetic in rapidly-varying fields, even when the frequency is over 100,000,000 per second "—and, as the result of the work described in the second paper, " the iron did not take more than $\frac{1}{10000}$ of a second for the rearrangement of the molecules into their final position, so that there is no appreciable time-effect in the demagnetization of finely-laminated iron ". It is clear from the wording of these conclusions that, in detail, the experiments had to do directly or indirectly with effects occurring in very short intervals of time, and it is probably correct to say that the most surprising part of a very singular achievement was the way in which Rutherford was able to estimate directly such small fractions of a second as were involved in this work. The " time apparatus ", to which he had already devoted some thought during his year as an honours student in the physics laboratory, was essentially a mechanical contrivance of levers and falling weights of great simplicity. But, by careful attention to details, it was made to give good results.

During the course of the first of the two papers already mentioned, we come upon the general remark, " It has been shown how a magnetized steel needle placed in a small solenoid may be used as a detector of an oscillatory discharge, and also as a means of determining the rate of decay of the oscillation." This was the starting point from which Rutherford began to take a practical interest in the transmission and detection of electromagnetic, Hertzian—or, as we should now say, " wireless "—waves. In 1887 Hertz had been the first to show that effects were radiated into space from suitable electrical systems in which rapidly alternating currents were produced—and that these effects were of the type previously predicted by Maxwell. He had detected the effects at a distance, by observing the minute spark which passed between two points in a " receiving " system. Now, in his main experiment, Rutherford had used that part of Hertz's apparatus which corresponds to the modern transmitter, merely because he was interested—as we have already seen— in rapidly alternating currents, and because this apparatus provided the most rapid alternations available. But, with his realization that " a magnetized steel needle . . . may be used as a detector of an oscillatory discharge ", the possibility of investigating the actual transmission of electromagnetic waves presented itself, and, in his last year in New Zealand, he was able to send and receive signals over the length of the physics laboratory. Moreover, he had in this work a ready-made subject for further research when he arrived in Cambridge in the autumn of 1895.

The possibility of further study abroad came to Rutherford through the award of an 1851 Exhibition Science Scholarship on the results of the researches which we have already described. Once every two or three years one of these scholarships was assigned to the university of New Zealand, and a recommendation to it was made after the candidates' original dissertations had been reported upon by referees in England. The successful scholar received £150 a year, for two— or perhaps three—years, in the university to which he elected to go. As the result of the competition in 1894, in which Rutherford was a candidate, J. S. Maclaurin, of Auckland, was the first to be nominated. Maclaurin had taken first-class honours in chemistry in 1892 and had therefore been one year longer at research than Rutherford had been. But, for family reasons, Maclaurin was unable to take up his award. Rutherford then became, as second choice, the first New Zealand student to be awarded an 1851 Exhibition scholarship in physics, and his own choice of Cambridge as the scene of his future investigations has already been indicated. On 7th August, 1895, it is recorded that two papers of his were the first two papers on the agenda of the Philosophical Institute of Canterbury, at Christchurch: eight weeks later he wrote in the cover of a small sixpenny notebook, " E. Rutherford, Cavendish Lab., Oct. 3, '95 ". If, in fact, he was present in person for the reading of the papers, he cannot have wasted much time, other than in travelling, in these eight weeks!

CHAPTER 3

Cambridge, the First Period, 1895-1898

WHEN, making his application to the Commissioners for the 1851 Exhibition Scholarship, Rutherford chose the Cavendish Laboratory at Cambridge as the scene of his further researches in physics, it is probable that one reason in particular was uppermost in his mind. J. J. Thomson was director of the laboratory and Cavendish professor of experimental physics in the university. At this time Thomson was thirty-seven years old and had already held the professorship for ten years, being the third occupant of the chair. He had built up a research school of considerable distinction and had established his own reputation as a mathematical and experimental physicist of the same calibre as his predecessors, James Clerk Maxwell and John William Strutt, third Baron Rayleigh—each of whom, being an older man at the time of his election, had enjoyed international repute throughout his tenure of the chair. All three, Maxwell, Rayleigh, and Thomson, had made important contributions to electrical theory, but Thomson's genius was more akin to Maxwell's than to Rayleigh's in this respect. He had edited the third edition of Maxwell's *Treatise* [1] and had written what amounted to a very voluminous supplement to it, bearing the title *Recent Researches in Electricity and Mag-*

---

[1] Quoted on p. 12

netism, and published in 1893. This had not long been published when Rutherford began his researches in New Zealand, and it had made a great impression on him, being frequently quoted in the two papers in the *Transactions of the New Zealand Institute* which we have already discussed.

Rutherford, then, elected to work at the Cavendish Laboratory—and he chose to enter Trinity College, when he became a member of the university. We need not delay further at this stage to inquire into the reasons for this latter choice; we shall merely remark that the three Cavendish professors up to Rutherford's time had all been members of Trinity College.

About the time that Rutherford chose Cambridge as the scene of his work, another development increased the attractiveness of this English university to the overseas student. A decision was taken which permitted the granting of degrees for research. For a great many years German universities had granted such degrees and had attracted large numbers of English, American, and Colonial students in consequence; now Cambridge was to enter into competition with them in this respect. On 18th June, 1895, a new statute concerning " advanced students " received the final sanction of the university authorities: nearly a year later (13th May, 1896) its provisions became effective when the approval of the Queen in Council was duly obtained. Perhaps because the deliberations of the syndicates appointed to draft the new statute had been protracted and wearisome, when success was finally achieved, those interested in the matter did not wait for the last rites of the formal procedure. We read " Advanced students are, as we learn, already in residence at Trinity and Christ's, if not elsewhere, waiting the full recognition that the university cannot give until the new statute has received the sanction of the Queen in Council." [1]   Rutherford was one of these advanced students. Actually, we are told, he was the first of them to be accepted and to begin serious work in the Cavendish Laboratory. Before the " full recognition " here spoken of was achieved, he had completed one substantial piece of research and had so far distinguished himself as to be chosen by his professor as a personal collaborator. Fourteen years later, compiling a history of the period for inclusion in a publication commemorating the twenty-fifth year of Thomson's professorship, Rutherford himself wrote, " At the beginning of the Easter term of 1896 Thomson was joined by Rutherford. . . ." [2]   Here it will be interesting to inquire into the genesis of this association of professor and research student which was to prove the beginning of one of the most remarkable periods of advance in the history of physical science.

During the ten years before Rutherford's arrival in Cambridge, much of the experimental work at the Cavendish Laboratory had been concerned with the passage of electricity through gases. Ordinarily, of course, matter in the gaseous state is non-conducting, but instances of exceptional conductivity, in the lightning discharge and the more modest spark which can be obtained from electrical machines in the laboratory, had been a well-known phenomenon since the beginning of the nineteenth century. Then, the development of the air pump led directly to further wide studies of gaseous conductivity. It was discovered that gas at low pressure might allow the passage of electricity when the same gas at ordinary atmospheric pressure did not

---

[1] *Cambridge Review*, 27th February, 1896.

[2] *A History of the Cavendish Laboratory*, 1910, p. 176.

—and it was found that luminosity was always associated with the conductivity. Gas-discharge tubes were therefore constructed in great variety and many strange and beautiful effects were obtained. About the year 1890 the study of these effects was beginning to pass from the purely descriptive to the strictly scientific phase. J. J. Thomson, in England, and Hertz, in Germany, along with their pupils, were largely responsible for this transition, which earlier work by Sir William Crookes had already initiated. In 1891 Thomson attempted to measure the velocity of propagation of the luminous effects associated with the electric discharge through the gas, and in 1894 he made a rough estimate of the velocity of motion of the cathode rays—a much discussed feature of the discharge which is particularly prominent at very low pressures. In 1892 Hertz had succeeded in obtaining effects outside the discharge tube indicating that these same cathode rays were able to penetrate thin sheets of metal. Two years later Lenard extended these observations. It was natural, therefore, that anyone arriving at the Cavendish Laboratory about this time should find plenty to interest him in this rapidly advancing subject. But Rutherford, as we know, had a problem of his own which was unfinished. To begin with, he continued this work on Hertzian waves, using the magnetic detector which he had already developed in New Zealand.

He worked quickly, and he was able to attract the interest of others, sufficiently, at least, to obtain their collaboration as occasion demanded. Gradually extending the range of his transmission, first from one end of the building to the other through intervening masonry, then across Jesus Common, a large open space near his lodgings, and finally from the laboratory to his lodgings, with half a mile of streets and houses between, he soon held the record for the time for long-distance transmission. But the mere attainment of distance did not appear to interest him greatly. He returned to other laboratory experiments using the magnetic detector, and, after many interesting investigations, in March, 1896, was still engaged on this work. In the middle of that month he made the following entry in his notebook:

" Monday Mch. 16. First Monday of Vac.
Vibrator in advanced room: receiver in my own room. Tried the effect of various needles with different magnetizing solenoids but with no very satisfactory results. Tried a specimen of chemically precipitated Fe_3O_4 but no effect at all: varied size of vibrator & distance between plates. . . . Left subject of vibrator & turned to experiments on screening effects of wires. . . ."

On the next page a few scattered figures give the results of these experiments on the screening effect—and that is the end. With the Easter vacation as a suitable transition period, Rutherford had clearly decided that the natural line of work of the laboratory offered more scope for his investigations—and his professor, too, had obviously decided that opportunities for his very evident genius ought certainly to be provided along that line: " At the beginning of the Easter term," therefore, " Thomson was joined by Rutherford." In the notebook no vacant space was left; facing the first fragmentary results of the screening experiment, on the opposite page is the heading " Note: Leakage of Electricity under action of X-rays ". These are the first jottings of ideas concerning the new line of work: in order to understand their full significance, and the urgency of the collaboration of professor and student which we are here discussing, we must again go back a few months in time and follow a train of events in physics which, starting in November, 1895, within the span of a hundred days plunged all the physical laboratories of Europe into feverish activity.

In November, 1895, Professor W. C. Röntgen of Würzburg announced the discovery of X-rays. Whilst operating a discharge tube in which the cathode rays were strongly developed, he discovered an effect outside the tube of quite a different order from that previously observed by Hertz and by Lenard. In his case no thin metal window was needed to allow the effective agent to escape from the tube, nor was its range of action limited to a few centimetres of air as before, but photographic plates were affected, even though shielded by considerable thicknesses of matter. Under suitable conditions, shadow photographs of metal objects, and of such structures as the bones of the hand, could be obtained. The effective agent, referred to as X-radiation in the original paper, appeared to originate in that portion of the wall of the discharge tube which was rendered phosphorescent under the action of the cathode rays. Röntgen himself fully appreciated the importance of his discovery, and the general public became suddenly aware, as it had never previously been aware, of the impact of pure scientific research on its everyday life. Reviewing this early period at a later date, Rutherford wrote, " It is difficult to realize to-day the extraordinary interest excited in the lay and scientific mind alike by the discovery of the penetrating X-rays. . . ." [1] Everyone with any facilities at all, from the veriest amateur

[1] *A History of the Cavendish Laboratory*, 1910, p. 175.

to the Cavendish professor, immediately turned his attention to these strange phenomena. Within a few weeks, experiments were in progress in the Cavendish Laboratory regarding the properties of the radiation; within a year, more than a hundred communications had been made to the learned societies of the world dealing with this particular subject. On the mathematical side Thomson was soon at work developing a suggestion which Röntgen had put forward concerning the nature of the radiation, and on 27th January, 1896, he presented his calculations to the Cambridge Philosophical Society, at their first meeting of the New Year. Certain experiments were demonstrated at the meeting, and on the very next day a new and most important effect was observed. With the help of McClelland, Thomson found that gases at ordinary pressures were rendered temporarily conducting under the influence of the radiation. This was a far-reaching discovery: previously, even at low pressures, large differences of potential were necessary before the conducting state was reached; under the influence of X-rays, however, gaseous conductivity began in the smallest electric fields.

Thomson communicated these results to the Royal Society at their meeting in London on 13th February, 1896, and great interest was aroused. In the course of the discussion he said

" The passage of these rays through a substance seems thus to be accompanied by a splitting up of its molecules, which enables electricity to pass through it by a process resembling that by which a current passes through an electrolyte."

Here was an hypothesis: it remained only to set to work to test its validity. To that test Rutherford began to devote his attention after the Easter vacation, as we have already indicated. His first note on the subject shows that he had already thought deeply on the problems involved; it begins

> " If 2 plates be taken one connected to earth and the other charged to a definite potential, under the action of X-rays, the potential rapidly falls, the rate of leak varying with the distance between the plates. The peculiarity is that the rate of leak increases with the distance between the plates although the electromotive intensity is much less. It seems as if. . . ."

From the very start, an important point is seized upon securely (the peculiarity here mentioned had not at the time been reported in the literature) and followed up with the persistence of genius. The note which we have quoted goes on to extend Thomson's hypothesis in order to " explain " the effect which had appeared so surprising: it is not very pertinent to our present story to report that the extension was not, in the upshot, a successful one—it was soon abandoned when further experiments afforded more extensive data for comparison. Throughout the summer Thomson and Rutherford were engaged on these experiments, and, by the time that the British Association met in September, they were able to present a picture of the processes occurring in a conducting gas in which all essential details were correct. The Association met in Liverpool, and Thomson, as it happened, was president of Section A. Referring, in advance, to the subject, in his presidential address, he said,

> " Mr. Rutherford and I have lately found that the conductivity is destroyed if a current of electricity is

sent through the Röntgenized gas. . . . When a current is passing through a gas exposed to the rays, the current destroys and the rays produce the structure which gives conductivity to the gas; when things have reached a steady state the rate of destruction by the current must equal the rate of production by the rays."

This is an exact but cautious statement; for the next year Rutherford was engaged in examining in detail precisely what this " structure which gives conductivity to the gas " might be.

Thomson's presidential address was delivered on Thursday 17th September. On Friday, 18th September, five papers on X-rays were read, and on the Saturday morning there were two further papers on the same subject. There could be no doubt what was the topic of the year in physics in 1896! Even so, on Monday, 21st September, Rutherford, returning to his old researches, presented an account of " A magnetic detector of electrical waves ". He had given a similar account to the Royal Society in the previous June and he had written up the work for publication. Twenty-seven years later the British Association again visited Liverpool, and, by a strange coincidence, Rutherford was president (1923). It was only natural that he should not let slip the opportunity for reference to the earlier occasion. He said,

" The visit to your city in 1896 was for me a memorable occasion for it was here that I first attended a meeting of this Association, and here that I read my first scientific paper . . . a paper which I had the honour to read, on a new magnetic detector of electrical waves. . . ."

We may think, perhaps, that we can detect here the subjugation of exact truth to the demands of courtesy; if so it is interesting to remark that the paper on the magnetic detector, written up for the *Transactions of the Royal Society*, also omits completely any mention of the fact that the work was a continuation of research begun in New Zealand—upon which, as we have seen, papers had already been read before a branch of the New Zealand Institute during the two previous years.

We have previously referred to the enormous output of—mostly qualitative—work on the production and properties of X-radiation during the year 1896. It so happened that what originally appeared to be a small side-issue in certain of these investigations led directly to a further discovery of equal importance with Röntgen's own. Henri Becquerel stumbled upon the first manifestations of the phenomenon of radioactivity in a way which we must now describe. Becquerel was present on 20th January, 1896, when the French Academy of Sciences received from Röntgen, through Poincaré, the first X-ray photographs to be seen in Paris. In the ensuing discussion he raised the question of the point of origin of the X-rays in the discharge tube, and was told that they appeared to originate in a patch of phosphorescence on the glass wall of the tube, where the cathode rays fell. He afterwards wrote,[1]

> " I immediately thought of looking to see whether . . . all phosphorescent substances emit similar (penetrating) rays . . . and on the next day I began a series of experiments. . . ."

For nearly a month these experiments produced only negative results. If certain information which Thomson

[1] *Recherches sur une propriété nouvelle de la matière*, 1903, p. 3.

had by this time obtained had been known to Becquerel, this would not have appeared as at all surprising; Thomson had already shown that it was possible to produce phosphorescence, even in the glass of the discharge tube, without obtaining any X-radiation. However, towards the end of February, Becquerel observed a number of effects apparently of the kind he was looking for. Fifteen years previously he had prepared some very fine crystals of a complex chemical compound, a double sulphate containing the metals potassium and uranium, and, when he recovered these crystals from a colleague, to whom he had lent them for an entirely different purpose some time previously, he at once found that, during exposure to sunlight, they emitted a penetrating radiation which was able to affect a photographic plate completely enclosed in black paper. He communicated this first successful achievement to the Academy of Sciences on Monday, 24th February, 1896—and pressed forward with his experiments. But February, in Paris, is hardly a month in which experiments requiring bright sunshine over long periods are most profitably performed: on Wednesday and Thursday, 26th and 27th February, the sun was visible only intermittently; on the next two days it was not seen at all. The apparatus was put by, in a drawer, to await a more favourable opportunity. Then, on Sunday, 1st March, by happy fortune, Becquerel decided to develop the photographic plates in spite of the lack of sunshine, so that at least he might have a negative control experiment to report at the weekly meeting of the Academy on the following day. To his great surprise he found a very intense photographic impression on examining his plates. After telling the members of the Academy of this result, he proceeded

to make further more definite tests, which confirmed
his conclusions, and by the next week he was able to
report that the crystals of potassium uranyl sulphate
appeared to emit continuously, without previous exposure to sunlight, radiations which not only affected
a photographic plate but also caused the leakage of
electricity from insulated bodies, just as the X-radiation
of Röntgen did. Moreover, he was able to report that
he had obtained similar effects with other salts of uranium. A new property of matter was certainly in
question—and it can only be attributed to the complete
preoccupation of most physicists in following up Röntgen's discovery, that Becquerel remained, for nearly a
year, practically the sole worker in an equally promising
field of inquiry. The position did not change until
Rutherford took up the study of the " electrical effects
of uranium potassium sulphate "—to make a further
quotation from his notebook—and embarked on a careful
quantitative comparison of the conductivity produced in
a given gas by the uranium radiation with that produced
in the same gas by the X-radiation from a discharge
tube. By the time that the full results of this detailed
comparison had finally been published, in January, 1899,
the subject of radioactivity was already attracting widespread attention—and Rutherford himself had clearly
decided that its investigation offered just the kind of
opening which his own powers as an experimenter most
required. As events proved, he was not mistaken in this
decision: with hardly any interruption he was engaged
on research in radioactivity for the rest of his life.

It is probable that Rutherford first began to look
into the question of the electrical effects of the uranium
radiation in the Lent term, 1897—at any rate, by the
time that he was due to report to the Commissioners

for the Exhibition of 1851 Scholarship, in the June of that year, he was able to announce that work on this subject was already in progress. Along with his report, Rutherford submitted an application for the renewal of his scholarship for a third year. If he were reappointed, he stated, he intended to apply himself to " further research on the conduction of electricity through gases, especially with regard to uranium radiation ". His professor wrote, strongly supporting the application, " he is quite in the first rank of physicists. . . . If it is not contrary to the rules to renew his Scholarship, I am sure such a proceeding would tend greatly to the advancement of Physical Science." The Commissioners, with such testimony before them, could scarcely do otherwise than accede to the request; even if they had not done so it is extremely unlikely that means would not have been found to keep Rutherford in Cambridge for the extra year. In December, 1897, he was awarded the Coutts Trotter studentship at Trinity College, with a tenure of two years from that date.

With considerable justice, the year 1897 may be regarded as marking the beginning of the first great period of Rutherford's achievement as an experimenter. Turning over the pages of his notebooks, even now, the excitement of discovery cannot fail to be aroused in the imagination of the reader; clearly the Rutherford of those days was never content with a single experiment, or an isolated line of approach to the solution of a problem. The whole subject of gaseous conduction was for him of uniformily absorbing interest; in rapid succession he investigated the different effects produced by X-rays, by ultra-violet light, and by the radiations from uranium, varying the conditions, day by day, now examining this, now that, aspect of the phenomenon.

Gradually, everything was reduced to order; the original picture which Thomson and he had formed of the mechanism of the conduction, and the mode of its excitation, proving itself fully able to explain all the results which were obtained. This was the position towards the end of the Lent term, 1898. As regards the constitution of the uranium radiation, however, and the wider problem of the nature of radioactivity in general, it was clear that much more remained to be done. This was the next step in Rutherford's achievement—and this we shall presently proceed to describe.

There is one thing, however, which must come before the next step is reached—another discovery of first-rate importance, made whilst Rutherford was fully occupied with the work which we have just been describing, which must be reported here as a necessary part of the background of our story. In later years, almost all the announcements of fundamental discoveries in physics were to come from Rutherford himself; it was his fate—and perhaps also his good fortune—that during his residence in Cambridge three such discoveries should have been made just beyond the bounds of his own achievement at the moment. We have already dealt with two of them, the discoveries of X-rays and of the radio-activity of uranium; the third, the isolation of the electron, was in large measure the work of Thomson in the Cavendish Laboratory in 1897. Early in that year Thomson was able to show that in discharge tubes filled with a wide variety of gases, at low pressures, the cathode rays had identical properties, so long as the difference of potential between the electrodes was the same in all cases. These rays behaved in every respect as if they were nega- tively charged corpuscles, much less massive than the lightest of all the atoms, the atom of hydrogen, in rapid

motion. They appeared to be fragments of atoms liberated under the action of the intense electrical forces in the
discharge tube—and, what was most important, fragments of the same type from whatever atom they were
obtained. The first clear evidence of a common structure
of matter, more fundamental than the differences in
chemical nature which .provided the usual basis of
classification, was thus perceived. For almost twenty
years it had been the usual belief amongst scientists on
the continent of Europe that the cathode rays would
prove to be an aetherial radiation, generally similar in
character to ordinary light, but even there, slightly
earlier even than Thomson, Wiechert and Kaufmann were
obtaining results which pointed to the corpuscular hypothesis. These investigations were indeed most important
initial steps in the general advance of knowledge at the
time, but, through a variety of circumstances, it was
rather Thomson's own work in Cambridge, multiplying
the many instances in which the so-called corpuscles
could be obtained, which really showed that a previously
unrecognized fundamental particle, a common constituent of all matter, had in fact been discovered. It is
interesting to record the remarkable penetration of
Thomson's physical insight in this connexion. His own
experiments gave no certain indication of the mass of
the corpuscles—merely indicating the mass per unit
charge by which they were characterized—yet he saw
clearly that, if the cathode rays were to be regarded as
material particles at all, the fact of their transmission
through thin metal foils and measurable thicknesses of
air, which Lenard had established, was incomprehensible
unless the particles were of a previously unimagined
smallness. In his own words,[1]

[1] Royal Institution weekly meeting, Friday, 30 April, 1897.

" Thus, from Lenard's experiments on the absorption of the rays outside the tube, it follows on the hypothesis that the cathode rays are charged particles moving with high velocities, that the size of the carriers must be small compared with the dimensions of ordinary atoms or molecules."

Thomson went on to remark,

" The assumption of a state of matter more finely subdivided than the atom of an element is a somewhat startling one. . . ."

nevertheless this assumption became an accepted part of physical theory, almost from the date of its inception.

Something further must now be said concerning Rutherford's own work on the uranium radiation, to which brief reference has already been made. Just as this work was beginning to enter on a most interesting phase, in the early summer of 1898, an entirely new situation arose for Rutherford himself. H. L. Callendar had resigned from the position of research professor at McGill University, Montreal, having been appointed head of the department of physics at University College, London. Callendar was only thirty-five years old and had been in Montreal for five years. During this time he had been elected Fellow of the Royal Society (in 1894) and had established a great reputation for himself. Naturally, the authorities were most desirous that a really promising successor should be found. The position was advertised and Rutherford was advised to apply. No doubt many weighty arguments suggested themselves both for and against taking action on this advice. The position of research professor was sufficiently uncommon to make the prospect decidedly attractive, apart from any other consideration, but the salary was not exceptional; Rutherford certainly looked forward to a professorship in the future, but, again, he was safely provided for, for at least another year, by the Trinity studentship. However, about the middle of May he decided to offer himself as a candidate, and on 30th of that month he completed his application, supported by testimonials from J. J. Thomson, Sir Robert Ball, Fellow of King's College and Professor of Astronomy, R. T. Glazebrook, Assistant Director of the Cavendish Laboratory, E. H. Griffiths, Fellow of Sidney Sussex College, W. W. Rouse Ball, his Tutor at Trinity, and a three-years-old testimonial from Bickerton, which had previously been used at the time of his entry to Cambridge. On 11th July, John Cox, head of the department of physics, together with the Principal of McGill University, interviewed Rutherford in Cambridge (Cox was himself a Trinity man— as also was Callendar) and the two men were able to appreciate at first hand the full measure of his reputation. They were not long in deciding to recommend his appointment—and this was confirmed from Montreal early in August. Then, on 8th September, Rutherford sailed from England to enter on his first professorship.

Since Rutherford's mind was deeply occupied with the turn of events in Montreal, it might be thought that his own research must necessarily have suffered from lack of attention during the summer of 1898. But no such effect can be detected in the results of his work. It was not his custom in those days to enter in his notebook the date of any particular series of observations, except very occasionally, but he did so when he started a new book on 24th February—he had not finished writing up the results of his last experiment for publication until three days previously—and the amount of work represented by the notes in this book, alone, shows that there was no slackening of effort during the following months. On 23rd August he sent in his final report to the Commissioners for the Exhibition of 1851 Scholarship, and on 1st September, just a week before he sailed, he submitted a full account of his experiments, as far as they had gone, for publication in the *Philosophical Magazine.* This account appeared in January, 1899, occupying fifty-five pages of print, and, in spite of the haste in which it must evidently have been put together, it may still be read with great profit as one of the classical descriptions of a pioneering experiment in physics. Concerning the much less detailed version of the work contained in the report to the Commissioners for the scholarship, a competent referee afterwards stated,

" I would not be expressing an exaggerated opinion in suggesting that the Commissioners may feel justly proud that it was through their scheme of science scholarships . . . that such a first-rate Physicist was enabled to come from New Zealand to the Cavendish Laboratory. . . ."

Rutherford had started work on the electrical properties of the uranium radiation with the knowledge that, like X-radiation, it rendered gases through which it passed electrically conducting—and with more than a suspicion that there were many other directions in which its effects were similar to those produced by the X-rays. His great achievement consisted in his showing that the essential characteristics of the conductivities produced by the two kinds of rays are, in fact, exactly —not merely approximately—the same, whilst at the same time appreciating certain minor differences which prevented him from adopting the too facile conclusion that the radiations themselves are of the same nature. Almost from the beginning he recognized these differences, and he persisted in his investigations until he was fully satisfied regarding their origin. It became clear to him that, entirely apart from the question of possible identity with the X-radiation, the radiation from uranium was not itself all of one kind. He wrote,[1]

> " These experiments show that the uranium radiation is complex and that there are present at least two distinct types of radiation—one that is very easily absorbed, which will be termed for convenience the α-radiation, and the other of a more penetrative character, which will be termed the β-radiation."

Rutherford may not himself have believed that he was distinguishing in this way two completely different physical agencies, but the truth of the matter is no less sensational than this, that a young student at the age of twenty-six years, in his first investigations, with a meagre amount of material, was so impressed with the different intensities of ionization produced near the surface of the material and a few centimetres away from the surface in air, that he suggested a distinction in terminology, the introduction of which has since been completely justified by a multitude of experiments. Six years later—for it was scarcely earlier than this—it had become an item of general scientific knowledge that the α- and β-radiations (the names are still employed) are in each case streams of fast-moving charged particles, but that the one type of particle is more than 7000 times as massive as the other—and that the charges are of opposite signs.

[1] *Phil. Mag.*, January, 1899, p. 116.

As regards the meagre amount of material available for these initial experiments, it is instructive again to quote from the original publication: [1]

" I did not, however, have enough uranium salt to test the variation of the rate of leak due to the β-radiation for thick layers."

This, no doubt, was strong reason for paying particular attention to the α-radiation, despite the fact that it was far less penetrating than the β-radiation, and that popular interest in a new radiation is apt to be directly proportional to its penetrating power. As we have stated, the effect of the α-radiation is completely cut off by a few centimetres thickness of air—and a single sheet of paper is equally effective. Nevertheless, Rutherford examined in detail the absorption of the radiation in different metals as well as in many gases, and never afterwards regretted his close study of what most people would normally have imagined at the time to be the least exciting of the new effects. As will in due course be recorded, in later years two out of the three completely outstanding discoveries associated with Rutherford's name were made using the α-radiations from radioactive materials.

Now that we have considered in some detail the chief experiments of the first Cambridge period, it is interesting to try to assess the main attributes of Rutherford's genius, which in Montreal was to fulfil so brilliantly its early promise. In this connexion we must recognize, above everything else, the conscious mastery with which his experimental method was always informed, and the strictly pioneering nature of all his work. Even his first New Zealand research, on the magnetic detector, was

[1] p. 119.

pioneering in the true sense of the term. He did not carry it beyond a certain point himself—and, at a later stage, he completely repudiated any interest in its commercial exploitation—but it is interesting to remark that, in purely academic research, the detector was used and developed by a number of workers. J. A. Erskine of Canterbury College, whose early association with Rutherford has already been mentioned (p. 26), spent the whole of his two years as 1851 Exhibition scholar, in Berlin and afterwards in Leipzig (1897–8), carrying out work with this instrument—and, later still, J. A. Pollock, professor of physics in Sydney, regularly reported progress with similar apparatus in yearly letters to Montreal. Certainly, as late as 1903, these investigations were still in progress: Pollock wrote,[1]

" We have had another active year with your detector though everything has turned out very tedious."

It might almost be claimed, for this original New Zealand research, that it initiated a distinct school of Australasian physics at the turn of the century; more-over, as far as Pollock is concerned, enlistment in this school seems to have taken place during the single day which Rutherford spent in Sydney on his journey to Cambridge in the autumn of 1895. Such is the slight contact with enthusiasm which sometimes suffices for inoculation.

The conscious mastery of the investigator exhibits itself in a number of ways: Rutherford not only carried out his experiments, but he sat in judgment on their reliability; he not only derived the obvious conclusions to which accepted methods of deduction inevitably led, but, in the form of asides to the main lines of argument,

[1] 17th March, 1903.

he would frequently add guesses of his own—utterances carrying the apparent assurance of intuitive knowledge, though assuredly they were not of this nature. Occasionally, as one would expect, they were mistaken. A characteristic example of a scientific guess—a conclusion unsupported by direct experimental evidence—occurs in the first New Zealand paper,[1]

" On account of the small quantity of electricity set in motion the experiments were not pursued further, but I have no doubt that by the use of very thin steel wires iron may be shown to be strongly magnetic for the highest frequencies yet obtained."

Several similar examples are to be found in the long paper on the uranium radiation of January, 1899. To quote one of these will be sufficient for our purposes at this stage: [2]

" I have been unable to observe the presence of any secondary radiation produced when uranium radiation falls on a metal. Such a radiation is probably produced, but its effects are too small for measurement."

Any ordinary student would have deserved censure for straying so far beyond the limits of what was actually ascertained: with Rutherford, perhaps, it did not appear so reprehensible.

His method of expressing judgment on the reliability of his experiments remained with Rutherford as an idiosyncrasy which was unaltered throughout life. In the margin of the page next following that which is reproduced in plate 2—the record, it will be remem-

[1] p. 509.   [2] p. 163.

bered, of his first essay in post-graduate research—against one particular paragraph occurs the simple, but utterly final, remark, " No good." This remark occurs again and again in notebooks of later years, and is still to be found amongst the sheaves of pencilled calculations and results which belong to the last period of all. Sometimes, of course, a favourable judgment is similarly recorded—" Good ", or " Very accurate experiment," or " Electrometer working very accurately." Rutherford knew which results to trust, it seems; for him there was never the recourse to the tedium of " the combination of observations " or " the weighted mean ". To this extent his was a dangerous method of prosecuting research—yet the outcome was almost always a strangely victorious advance into new territories of knowledge.

Already well in the forefront of progress in fundamental research, Rutherford lost no opportunity during his stay in Cambridge of improving his knowledge of the foundations of his science. In New Zealand, through the medium of the printed page, he had acquired a distant familiarity with the names of the great; now he was able to meet many of them in person, or count them his teachers. Besides Thomson, whose title to fame, in spite of his lack of years, we have already discussed, England—and often Cambridge, too—could at that time boast of Stokes, Kelvin, Routh, Crookes, Dewar, Rayleigh and Lodge. Stokes, at nearly eighty, was still lecturing on optics to advanced students; Lodge, much the youngest on our list, was approaching his fiftieth year.[1] Rutherford must have been particularly impressed by this great concourse of genius—and by

[1] Five of the seven men of science mentioned here lived to be over eighty years old; Routh, at seventy-six, died the youngest of them all. In the list, as given above, the names stand in the order of age.

its longevity, one outstanding example of which must certainly be quoted as belonging to our subject. On 9th November, 1896, Stokes communicated his theory of X-rays to the Cambridge Philosophical Society—fifty-four years after he had first addressed that society on a scientific topic! It was a great achievement for a man of seventy-seven years to put forward a theoretical explanation of a new phenomenon in physics which was destined to be accepted as essentially correct by all subsequent workers. Undoubtedly Rutherford would be amongst those present at this meeting; equally certainly he would be quick to appreciate its full significance. The deep respect which he developed for scientists of former generations was thus no baseless sentimentalism. It never brought him to the mock-modesty of Newton—"If I have seen farther it is by standing on the shoulders of giants," [1] but it remained with him to the end, so that, long after he personally had come to be accounted one of the ancients, he wrote to Lord Rayleigh,[2]

> "I am sure that we all ought to . . . give some of our recollections of those past and gone before they are lost for good. I am always surprised to find how little the younger generation knows about these matters. They have the impression that Science only started in their time!"

It may be that the vision of that younger generation, of which he wrote, would have appeared less bedazzled by contemporary achievement, to a Rutherford who had not himself outshone the brilliance of his predecessors. Or, again, since the young men whom he had

[1] Newton to Hooke, 2nd February, 1676.
[2] 5th March, 1936.

in mind in this denunciation were, most of them, his own pupils, he might almost have forgiven them the myopia of discipleship!

So much has already been said of the great interest with which the early work of Rutherford was received in the world of science, that something ought also to be added concerning the reception which his discoveries were accorded in the non-scientific academic society in Cambridge, and in the world generally. Naturally there were many, especially amongst the non-scientists in the university, who had doubted gravely the wisdom of the new regulations, which admitted students from other universities—even from the smallest and most recent foundations in the dominions—to a Cambridge degree on the result of two years research. But, if immediate justification of the scheme had been desired by its sponsors, it could hardly have been launched at a more opportune time. Physics, as we have seen, was on the threshold of great developments, and Rutherford, the first of the advanced students, was of precisely the type of young scientist who would not only make the most of his opportunity, but also improve upon it by his own achievement. It was not surprising, therefore, that, before long, the fame of his doings should have spread beyond the four walls of the laboratory, and have become a topic of discussion in senior common-rooms, or on the towpath.

But such fame did not come entirely without disillusionment—which happened once in this way. One day Rutherford received an invitation to a luncheon party—and an invitation to come early. Rumours of the new physics, it appeared, had begun to be heard even in the last stronghold of the littérateur, and Oscar Browning himself had begun to feel the need to be acquainted—and to see that some of his friends were similarly acquainted—with the findings of experiment in this particular direction. So he had issued this unconventional invitation. Rutherford accepted, and kept his appointment. For half an hour, before the others were due to arrive, his host bombarded him with questions regarding his work and its implications. For Rutherford, no doubt, it was flattering to find such interest in a senior member of the university, of such eminence, whose subject was so remote from his own. But, the party being assembled and the meal served, events moved to less certain flattery. Rutherford sat spellbound and astonished, as his host delivered himself of a magnificent discourse on the subject of his very recent enlightenment, with hardly so much as a passing reference to the person of his informant, or to his contributions to the subject under discussion. It was a slightly puzzled estimate of the attitude of the literary " don " that Rutherford took with him from that meeting. It is certain that he had not forgotten the incident when he himself became a member of that same class of being, on his return to Cambridge as Cavendish professor, more than twenty years later.

During his years as a research student, Rutherford did not frequently find himself straying far beyond the associations of science, or the bonds of a common colonial origin, in his social contacts. Throughout the week, it was mostly work in the laboratory; at the week-ends, walking or cycling, and the company of fellow New Zealanders, or of an Australian, perhaps, like Elliot Smith—or no company at all, except his own. From his lodgings, where his living-room was adorned with a multitude of photographs of his home and his old college at Christchurch, he wrote regularly to

Taranaki, long letters to his mother. They were un-rhetorical letters, naïve at times, yet never extravagant, always critical, even to the point of a certain insensibility to traditional things—which, in one who had grown up in a young country, was not, after all, altogether surprising. Thus, of the Great Gate of Trinity, he wrote,

> " The entrance is not very imposing—a narrow archway and then a big grass enclosure with college rooms all round—old and antiquated in appearance,"

and, of the villages which he found on his excursions into the country,

> " One comes across some very old villages with mud and stone houses, thatched and very dilapidated . . .";

of one, whose textbooks he had used and admired, and now met in the flesh,

> " . . . a small bullet-headed, decidedly commonplace man with no distinctive air of any kind,"

and, of the undergraduates,

> " The university here takes a tremendous lot of care of the undergraduates. They are kept very restricted and well bound down by rules."

Even the laboratory was not as well fitted up as he expected. In this matter, however, a healthy realism soon reasserted itself:

> " The more I see of the Laboratory the better I am pleased with it . . . it has a fine collection of instruments."

For the periods of long vacation residence, Rutherford moved into rooms in college, as undergraduates still do, even though they spend the rest of the year in lodgings. It is evident from his letters that he enjoyed the experience more perhaps than his first glimpse of the " old and antiquated " court led him to expect. " My study is a very large room 22 × 22 feet, but with a rather low ceiling," he wrote, " . . . it is fine and cool in this hot English weather."

During just such a spell of college life he wrote the proudest of all his early letters. On 4th August, 1898, he began, " I know you will all be pleased to hear that I have got the Montreal post. . . ." But that reflection brings us again to the end of a period; the rest of that letter belongs properly to the next chapter of this book.

CHAPTER 4

Montreal, 1898-1907

THE proud letter, just quoted, continues:
    " . . . and so [I] start up in life as a professor
on £500 a year . . . and an unlimited prospect of
work . . . it is as good an opening for a start as I
could wish. . . . The salaries are small compared
with the endowment of the laboratories and the
enormous money spent on them, but that is chiefly
due to the fact that the money has been advanced
by Macdonald, a millionaire who made his money
in tobacco and he lives on £250 a year, so he reckons
a professor should live on £500. However, £500 is
not so bad and as the physical laboratory is the best
of its kind in the world, I cannot complain."

Through all this rationalization an instinctive grasp of
the situation is clear. Behind and above pure reason,
obviously the scientist in Rutherford is saying " Radioactivity is something essentially and fundamentally
new; give me a laboratory of my own, efficient collaboration and good resources, and let us see what its
nature is." Montreal provided the perfect opportunity:
we shall not need to wait long in order to discover what
good use Rutherford made of it.

Naturally, it was not given to everyone to see the
possibilities, from the first, in the way that Rutherford
saw them: his parents wrote wondering if he had done

wisely—he had another year at Trinity in hand, and there was the chance of a new chair at £700 a year at home in New Zealand. But the reply had been simple,

> " Even if there had been a physical chair at £700, I would sooner have gone to Montreal at £500, as the laboratory is so much finer."

He had made up his mind, and when McGill University opened its doors, late in September, 1898, he was already busy about his new laboratory. A day or two before he left England he had received a farewell letter from the Master of Trinity, H. M. Butler, which, judged by after events, seems strangely prophetic,

> " Perhaps some day the same wave that has restored Professor Callendar to us may bring you also back over the Atlantic. Meanwhile, you will be doing a grand work in Canada, as the representative of other good things besides your own splendid subject."

It was clear that his course of action did not seem grossly improvident to all those who were in a position to advise him.

A day or two before he left England, also, Rutherford ordered, through the secretary at the Cavendish Laboratory, some uranium and thorium salts with which to continue his work on radioactivity. On 24th October, 1898, he wrote reminding the secretary of this order and asking that the material should be forwarded as soon as it arrived. Even with new duties to be assimilated, he was obviously keen to get down to his own work at the earliest opportunity, and was impatient when apparently cut off from supplies by three thousand miles of ocean. The cause of his impatience appears some years later in a letter to his mother (5th January, 1902),

" I have to keep going, as there are always people on my track. I have to publish my present work as rapidly as possible in order to keep in the race. The best sprinters in this road of investigation are Becquerel and the Curies in Paris, who have done a great deal of very important work in the subject of radio-active bodies during the last few years."

From the very beginning, this urge to be in the race—to be ahead in the race—was an all-powerful force in his life. In May, 1899, a paper entitled " Thorium and uranium radiation " was communicated to the Royal Society of Canada, and, by the end of the year, two more detailed accounts of researches in radioactivity had been sent off to England for publication to a wider public. From that instant, for the next eight years, there was never further question, but, by universal admission, the Macdonald Physics Laboratory at Montreal led the world in investigations into this particularly interesting new field of physical research.

But, before we go on to consider the achievements of the Montreal period, we must first make closer acquaintance with the two new sprinters from Paris mentioned in the quotation above. For Pierre and Marie Curie were, beyond question, pioneers in radioactivity in the same class of eminence as Rutherford himself. Pierre was thirty-six and Marie twenty-eight when Becquerel announced the discovery of the radioactivity of uranium in 1896; also, they had quite recently been married (1895). As Rutherford had done, for a number of years the Curies had worked chiefly at the subject of magnetism—Pierre being already recognized as an authority in this field—and Marie was actively engaged in the preparation of a monograph on the properties of various types of magnet steel, at the time we are considering. This was published in 1897 by the Society for the Encouragement of National Industry.

After Becquerel's discovery, the Curies interrupted their magnetic researches and began a systematic study of a large number of minerals, to see whether any of them might turn out to be radioactive which did not contain uranium. In April, 1898, after a long search, they announced to the Paris Academy of Sciences that thorium minerals, alone, of all that they had investigated, were of this nature—and then, in July and December of the same year, supplemented this announcement by two others of a much more startling nature. Actually, in the discovery of the thorium radioactivity they had been anticipated by a few weeks by G. C. Schmidt, who was working in Erlangen, but these later more important discoveries were peculiarly their own. They concerned nothing less than the existence of previously unknown chemical species of which the radioactivity was enormously greater, weight for weight, than the radioactivity of uranium or thorium. Observations and conclusions proceeded as follows. Tested under identical conditions, certain uranium minerals were found to be more active than metallic uranium itself. In any case a surprising result, this became important and exciting in relation to Becquerel's earlier proof that artificially prepared salts of uranium were active in proportion to the amount of uranium which they contained (see p. 45). For the earlier result established radioactivity as an atomic, rather than a molecular, property—and the Curies' observation could then only imply that the more active natural minerals contained, as chemical " impurity ", one or more previously unknown atomic types of very great activity.

Impelled by the logic of this conclusion, and encouraged by the failure of all attempts to produce abnormally active mixtures by trying to reproduce the chemical composition of the minerals in question, Pierre and Marie Curie began their search for the new elements. They took over a disused shed as a laboratory, and set to work on the analysis of a ton or so of uranium residues with which they had been presented by the Austrian government from the state mine at Joachimsthal. Their communication to the Academy of Sciences in July, 1898, told of the first success in this analysis— the separation of an active substance along with the bismuth contained in the mineral. In honour of Poland, the country of her birth, Marie Curie suggested the name " polonium " for the active element here concerned. The December communication, which bore the name of Bémont, as collaborator with the Curies, told of the second success, the recognition of another active element, chemically allied to barium, to which the name " radium " was given. Within six months, therefore, two " new " chemical elements had been shown to exist—and, it might be added in parenthesis, that the tests, by which the concentration of each was followed in the process of purification, were entirely physical ones, the ionization produced by the emitted radiations being determined, at each stage of the process, rather than the effective combining weight of the mixture, or any other of its chemical properties.

This was the position at the end of 1898. In the following year many chemists naturally turned their attention to the new field of inquiry—though, equally naturally for us, any attempt to follow their researches here must be abandoned as entirely impracticable. But two results of the Curies might be added, as of exceptional interest. Continuing their analysis, by attempts to separate polonium from bismuth and radium from barium, they eventually came to the conclusion that, although in the second case weighable amounts of a pure chemical substance could be obtained which was highly radioactive, in the former case no such pure substance could be obtained. Radium was thus " discovered " chemically, with a combining weight of about 113, but polonium remained, from the chemist's point of view, a hypothetical element. Moreover, the radioactivity of all polonium preparations slowly decayed with the passage of time. At the end of a year these preparations were less than half as active as they had been at the beginning.

In the light of the results which have just been set out, it hardly requires the testimony of Rutherford's early letter to his mother to render credible the assumption that the work of the Curies made a deep impression on his active mind—or provided a strong incentive to him to press forward with his own researches.

The two discoveries—of the radioactivity of thorium compounds and of the polonium activity—were made before Rutherford left Cambridge in the autumn of 1898. As we have already indicated (p. 63), he verified the former result for himself in the course of the summer of that year, noticing certain interesting facts to the elucidation of which he returned as soon as he was able to begin work again in Montreal. The announcement of the latter discovery, however, in its first impact on him, did not carry conviction as regards the interpretation offered by its authors. In his paper on the uranium radiation, aside from the main line of argument, Rutherford wrote (September, 1898), " It is possible that the apparently very powerful radiation obtained from pitchblende by Curie may be partly due to the very fine state of division of the substance rather than to the presence of a new and powerful radiating substance." [1] From the vantage-point of the present day, this suggestion certainly does not appear to bear the hall-mark of genius: rather does it run clean contrary to the established facts. Yet, when the balance is struck at the end of the Montreal period—or three or four years earlier, for that matter—there can be no doubt whence the greater outpourings of genius had sprung. During the course of this chapter, three topics, chosen from many others which formed the subjects of almost equally important investigations within the same period, will be touched on with such detail as restricted space may allow, and in each case, though important contributions will be seen to have come from Paris, or other European centres of research, the final experimental success or theoretical unification will appear without question as the work of Rutherford in Montreal. The topics chosen in this connexion are (i) the discovery and nature of the radioactive emanations, (ii) the nature of radioactive change, and (iii) the heating effects accompanying radioactivity. Although the assignment represents a great over-simplification of the position, because Rutherford always had several lines of investigation in operation at any single time, these topics may be said to have contributed his major interests in physics during the years 1899, 1901–2, and 1903, respectively.

The discovery of the radioactive emanations had its germ in the observation recorded in the first paper on the uranium radiation: "It was found that thorium nitrate when first exposed to the air on a platinum plate was not a steady source of radiation, and for a

[1] *Phil Mag..*, January, 1899.

time . . . varied very capriciously." [1] This remained
an isolated observation until Rutherford was able to
resume work in Montreal; then the original result was
confirmed and extended. The effect was found to be
even more notable with the oxide of thorium than with
the nitrate, and " was examined in detail as it was
thought it might possibly give some clue as to the
cause and origin of the radiation emitted by these
substances ". R. B. Owens, afterwards secretary of
the Franklin Institute in Philadelphia, and then Macdonald professor of electrical engineering at McGill
University, was planning a visit to the Cavendish
Laboratory for the summer of 1899, and, possibly as
an introduction to Cambridge physics, joined Rutherford in this investigation in the spring of that year.
But he had to leave for England before any clear idea
of the nature of the effect was obtained. By June,
however, the word " emanation " was beginning to
appear in Rutherford's notebooks, and, to judge from a
reply from J. J. Thomson,[2] it must have found its way
into his correspondence, also: about this time a working
hypothesis was evidently deepening into a strong conviction in his mind. By the middle of September he was
able to write the first full account for publication, at
the very beginning of the paper [3] setting forth his ideas
with entire clarity and great boldness: " In addition
to this ordinary radiation, I have found that thorium
compounds continuously emit radioactive particles of
some kind, which retain their radioactive powers for
several minutes ". It was in the sense of a gas-like
substance made up of these radioactive particles that

---

[1] *Phil. Mag.*, January, 1899.   [2] 23rd July, 1899.

[3] *Phil. Mag.*, January, 1900.

the name " emanation " had thus been brought into use. The inconstancy previously observed in the radiations from preparations of thorium oxide had been traced to the effects of air currents blowing over the surface of the solid material, and every aspect of this inconstancy had been shown to point to the fact of the steady evolution of minute amounts of a gaseous radioactive substance from the thorium compound, capable of being carried away by the currents of air. On the other hand, the attainment of a constant limiting activity when air currents were completely excluded, could only be explained, on the basis of a continuous production of radioactive gas, if the activity of the emanation itself was not constant, but decreased with the passage of time. This decrease was experimentally observed by transferring emanation-bearing air into a closed vessel and following the time rate of change of the ionization produced. The activity of the emanation was thus shown to diminish " in a geometrical progression with the time ", the intensity falling to half value after an interval of about one minute. Formally, at least, the whole phenomenon appeared to be satisfactorily explained. As regards the question whether the emanation particles were atomic in size or considerably larger—of the nature of dust particles—experiment appeared to speak in favour of the former alternative. The emanation seemed to behave in all respects like a true gas, always present in such minute amounts that its gaseous nature could not be inferred except from the way in which its ionizing activity might be moved about at will from one place to another.

Roughly speaking, such were the contents of Rutherford's first paper on the thorium emanation—a strange but a satisfactory beginning. As soon as he read the paper, H. L. Callendar wrote to Rutherford,[1]

"I see you are still working at those fascinating rays which promise so much insight into the nature of things."

In actual fact, even before these words were written, much of that promise had already been fulfilled, and Rutherford had sent a second and considerably longer paper to England for publication. Again, the utter directness of the first sentences almost startles the reader:

"Thorium compounds under certain conditions possess the property of producing temporary radioactivity in all solid substances in their neighbourhood. The substance made radioactive behaves . . . as if it were covered with a layer of radioactive substance like uranium or thorium . . . the intensity of the excited radiation is not constant, but gradually diminishes."[2]

Here, certainly, was another crop of experimental results challenging reasonable explanation in terms of accepted theories (or providing and promising "further insight into the nature of things", according to the philosophical outlook of the individual!). Although many of these results had been obtained before the first paper on the emanation was written—for Thomson's letter of 23rd July, 1899, refers to some of them—after briefest mention at the end of that paper they had been "reserved for a later communication". This was both cautious and also expedient—expedient because the

---

[1] 19th January, 1900.   [2] *Phil. Mag.*, February, 1900.

new results alone required a great deal of space for their presentation (the second paper eventually ran to thirty-two pages of print), and cautious because, although Rutherford believed the production of " excited radio-activity " to depend somehow upon the action of the emanation, he was not quite sure that the two effects were as directly connected as he supposed.

As he was putting the finishing touches to the new paper, the first evidence of similar results from Paris arrived in Montreal. Early in November, 1899, M. and Mme Curie announced their discovery of the production of " induced ", or excited, radioactivity on solid substances kept in the neighbourhood of strong radium preparations, and, although their explanation of the phenomenon did not coincide with his own, Rutherford recognized the essential identity of the two effects. It was a year or two before he satisfied himself completely as to the nature of the connexion, but the discovery of radium emanation by Dorn in the follow-ing year (1900), fortified his belief that the excited radioactivity in each case required the intermediary action of a radioactive emanation for its production. Thomson inclined to the view that this activity was due directly to condensed emanation:

" . . . the idea that I got on reading the experiments was that . . . the emanation . . . tended rather to condense round the positive ions than the negative ones, as we might expect an electro-positive substance to do," [1]

but for Rutherford the different rates of decay of activity (to half value in one minute for that due to the free

[1] 21st December, 1899.

emanation, and in about eleven hours for the excited activity, in the case of thorium) was sufficient disproof of this contention. He thought rather of the deposition of radioactive particles from the thorium compound on the activated surface, and, although he was clear that these particles were distinct from the particles of emanation, he recognized the great importance of the fact that they appeared only in those places to which particles of emanation had had access. We shall see, later in this chapter, how, in its essentials, this view afterwards proved to be correct—and how Rutherford himself supplied the ideas which resolved those obscurities which still remained with it at the time of which we write.

As we have mentioned, Rutherford's two papers on the thorium emanation and excited radioactivity were published in January and February, 1900. Here are three interesting indications of the effects which they had on physicists in different parts of the world. On 25th March, 1900, Zeleny wrote from the University of Minnesota,

" I read your papers with very great interest. I am about ready to believe that most anything is possible."

Zeleny had been a research student in Cambridge during the second and third years of Rutherford's period there, and the two men had formed a lasting friendship. Then, from Trinity College, Dublin, G. F. Fitzgerald wrote, on 5th May, 1900,

" We were very much interested in your thorium experiments. There seems no doubt that there is some emanation from the thorium. . . . I have got some thorium but we are all too lazy here to do

experiments and indeed between National Education
Boards, Veterinary College Boards, Technical School
Boards, etc., etc., one gets sick of doing anything."

Fitzgerald had previously been much impressed by
Rutherford's work on electric waves and had had correspondence with him on that subject. He was, of course,
considerably senior to Rutherford and Zeleny, and
died at the age of fifty in the following year. The third
letter came from R. J. Strutt (now Lord Rayleigh), and
was addressed from Cambridge. It read,

> " I have been trying to repeat your experiments on
> ' induced radioactivity ' without much success. . . .
> I think my thorium oxide must be in fault. . . . I
> am writing to ask if you could send me some thorium
> oxide which you know to be efficient."

Here, there is explicit trust in Rutherford's results, in
spite of personal failure to repeat them—and, in spite
of apparent superficiality, a correct suggestion in explanation of that failure. For previously—and he repeated the work in greater detail at a later date—
Rutherford had investigated the different types of
treatment which rendered thorium oxide poor or efficient
as a source of emanation and excited activity. Truly,
radioactivity was a subject for magicians, in those early
days.

So our first topic has been exhausted, and here,
before proceeding to the next, we may pause to recount
something of Rutherford's manner of life in Montreal,
of his friends, and of his first holiday in New Zealand
in the summer of 1900. For that holiday, too, marked
a great change in his life, as we shall presently discover.

When Rutherford arrived in Montreal, in September,

1898, he stayed for a short time at the home of H. T. Bovey, the dean of the faculty of Applied Science, until he moved into rooms in a boarding-house, close to the university, where E. W. MacBride also boarded. MacBride was professor of zoology at McGill (and afterwards professor of zoology at Imperial College, South Kensington), and he and Rutherford had been thrown together as fellow-travellers on the boat from Liverpool to Quebec. They remained together when, after a few months, their boarding-house closed; then they found new rooms for themselves in Union Avenue. Here they were joined by J. W. Walker, professor of chemistry in the university. In their new rooms breakfast was provided, but they had to take their meals out during the remainder of the day. Poor comfort for three university professors, one might think, but then one should remember Macdonald—and Rutherford's letter to his mother—in this connexion (p. 62).

Very soon the three professors who lodged together became the closest of friends and others, too, were admitted to their circle. More than twenty years later R. B. Owens wrote,

" It is a long time since we worked and played together at McGill, but I often recall those days very dear to me, and always with a feeling that warms my heart."

Serious young men, no doubt they were, but inconsequent and riotous also, after a fashion—as Rutherford often was riotous in laughter in later years. And, even his work, too, could not be expected to remain entirely beyond the bounds of this inconsequence. Since its whole fabric was informed by the driving enthusiasm and the strength of youth, it is not surprising that it was also, occasionally, touched by a freakish immaturity of wit. Thus for many years his own initials, " E. R.", were consistently used in his notebooks to denote " excited radioactivity ". (There is a highly rationalized —and, it must be admitted, convincingly rationalized— footnote in one of his later papers explaining his preference for " excited " rather than " induced " in this association!). And, in one notebook with numbered pages, when the experiment brought him eventually to page 99 in the book, apparently he was unable to resist the temptation to utilize the printed figures as part of the date, July, 7, 1899, although it was far from his invariable custom to make note of the date at all.

In the early summer of 1900, Rutherford left Montreal for New Zealand, travelling through the Western States and taking ship at San Francisco. Only twenty months had elapsed since he set foot in the dominion, and, looking back on that short time, the wonder is that he had achieved so much, rather than that he had omitted to do this thing or that. Certain things, of course, he had omitted to do. He had failed to keep up-to-date with all his correspondents across the Atlantic, one friend of Nelson College days complaining,[1]

" . . . you have never answered my last note written about 18 months ago—however . . . I have heard of you occasionally through roundabout ways—but strange to say the news . . . was only attenuated and not adulterated."

Then he failed, occasionally, even to give all the time to his experiments that they required:

[1] W. H. Dawson, 19th October, 1900.

" On account of the press of other work, it was not found possible to take observations at regular intervals, but the table given below suffices to show the general nature of the results." [1]

And, finally, if certain indications are correct, he must clearly have intended, originally, to return to New Zealand twelve months earlier than he did—and in this, too, he failed. For, in writing to bid him farewell when he set sail from England, Mrs. (now Lady) Thomson concluded,

" It sounds a very delightful arrangement to spend your next Long Vacation in your own country and return to Montreal married! I hope you will be able to manage it. . . . We send you and Miss Newton our very best wishes for all future happiness." [2]

Rutherford's engagement to Miss Mary Georgina Newton—they had been friends in his undergraduate days at Canterbury College—had been announced in 1896, and one of the chief reasons for his planning an early return to New Zealand was, in the words of Mrs. Thomson, that he might " return to Montreal married ". This he did in September, 1900, travelling by way of Honolulu, Vancouver and the Canadian Rockies. By the time that the undergraduates re-assembled for the beginning of the new academic year he was ready to resume work in the laboratory—and he was established in a home of his own in St. Famille Street.

When Rutherford returned to Montreal in 1900 he

[1] *Phil. Mag.*, February, 1900.   [2] 2nd September, 1898.

found that a young Oxford chemist, Frederick Soddy, had been appointed demonstrator in the chemistry department. Soddy was just twenty-three years old and, arriving early in Montreal, before the summer was over, had already made the acquaintance of Mac-Bride, who introduced him to Rutherford. This introduction proved to have the most far-reaching results. Early in 1901 Soddy abandoned such research as he was doing in the chemistry department and joined Rutherford in a physico-chemical attack on the problem of the radioactive emanation and other products of thorium. As we follow up this attack we shall find ourselves plunged straight into the discussion of the second scientific topic of our choice, the nature of radioactive change—and we shall find ourselves dealing with events which, in the upshot, confirmed, perhaps more fully than he had ever expected, the wisdom of Rutherford's early speculation. For the " clue as to the cause and origin of the radiation ", the most fundamental problem in the whole science of radioactivity, was in fact found in the detailed examination of the original thorium anomaly (p. 68).

Several possible ways suggest themselves in which we might attempt to assess the magnitude of this achievement of Rutherford and Soddy, before proceeding to details. First, there is evaluation by mere weight of numbers. This remarkable association of physicist and chemist lasted for just more than two years. It resulted in eight published papers covering nearly 150 pages of print, though with some repetitions—a twenty-page paper every three months of term and vacation, it might almost be reckoned. Secondly, there is Soddy's own explicit estimate at the end of the period,[1]

---

[1] 31st March, 1903.

" I mention this to show that we are on a flood-tide of interest and I do not want to delay."

And, finally, we are surely entitled to read a personal evaluation of their achievement in Rutherford's changing attitude towards his own position at McGill during the years under consideration. Thus, in March, 1901, before the work with Soddy had progressed beyond the exploratory stage, it was announced that P. G. Tait, at the age of seventy, was about to vacate the chair of Natural Philosophy in the university of Edinburgh, which he had held for more than forty years. Rutherford was attracted by this possibility of returning to a British university and wrote to Thomson for advice:[1]

" After the years in the Cavendish I feel myself rather out of things scientific. . . . I think this feeling of isolation is the great drawback to colonial appointments, for unless one is content to stagnate, one feels badly the want of scientific intercourse."

To this Thomson replied:[2]

" As I cabled to you I think you had better stand for the Edinburgh chair if you wish to return to England. I do not think the chances of your getting the post very promising . . . at the same time I think the candidature will do you good as it will let people know that you are willing to leave Montreal. . . ."

So Rutherford applied—and it was probably extremely fortunate for him, as events rapidly proved, that Thomson's prediction was verified: a much older man, J. G. Macgregor, who had been professor at Dalhousie College, Halifax, Nova Scotia, was appointed from a very

[1] 26th March, 1901.   [2] 12th April, 1901.

large field.   So the Rutherford-Soddy experiments went
forward—and, less than a year later, when Rutherford
had the chance of influential support for the position
of Callendar's successor at University College, London,
(Callendar had accepted the chair of physics at Imperial
College) he declined the offer.   E. H. Griffiths had
written to him,[1]

> " I have told them that it appears to me that the
> man who would most nearly fulfil their requirements
> would be yourself.   I am afraid, however, that you
> will not leave Montreal. . . ."

By this time, that indeed was the case: very soon there
was no longer the same feeling of isolation in this colonial
appointment, for all the adventurous young men who
wished to keep abreast of the latest work in the newest
and most exciting branch of physics made the journey
to Montreal themselves, to work under Rutherford's
direction.   And now, after this digression, it is necessary
for us to proceed again to details.

Five questions, recorded in full in their first paper,
soon " presented themselves for answer " when Rutherford and Soddy began work on the thorium emanation
in the spring of 1901.   Two of these questions, more than
the others, call for attention in the present account of
their work.   We may paraphrase them as follows:
(i) what is the chemical nature of the gaseous emanation?,
and (ii) is the emanation given off by thorium itself
or by some foreign substance present " possibly in
minute amount, associated with it and amenable to
chemical methods of separation "?   After subjecting
emanation-laden air to extreme heat and to such a

[1] 21st December, 1901.

degree of extreme cold as they were able to command, after bringing it in contact with chemical reagents of all types (substituting other gases for air when occasion demanded)—and finding that in every case the emanation passed unchanged through the test—they were able to offer what appeared to them a convincing answer to the first of these questions:

"the only known gases capable of passing in unchanged amount through all the reagents employed are the recently discovered gases of the argon family . . . the interpretation of the experiments must be that the emanation is a chemically inert gas analogous in nature to the members of the argon family." [1]

This is in itself an interesting conclusion. The gases of the argon family were discovered by Lord Rayleigh and Sir William Ramsay during the years 1894 to 1900, being recognized in the first place merely by density determinations. These gases being completely devoid of chemical properties, the fundamental property of weight provided the most ready means of their detection. But, as we have already remarked, weighable amounts of thorium emanation were never to be obtained in the work we are considering—whilst, in fact, more than a hundredweight of argon had remained undiscovered in the atmosphere above each square yard of the earth's surface until 1894. Yet, after a year or two of experiment, the emanation was recognized as a gas similar in nature to argon! Somewhile later, Soddy made the most of this comparison in a popular but informative article in the *McGill University Magazine*:

"A *gas* without properties is a somewhat intangible body to demonstrate the existence of. . . . But it

[1] *Trans. Chem. Soc.*, April, 1902.

would be impossible for a well-mannered electrometer to mistake uranium rays for thorium rays, or,
again, to confound the latter with those other rays
given out by the thorium emanation. By their rays
ye shall know them."

Concerning the second of the above questions, also,
very soon definite indications of an answer began to
appear. By a variety of chemical separations, at first
not easily repeatable, it was found possible to concentrate, in a small fraction of the original bulk, whatever
agents were responsible both for the production of
emanation by thorium compounds and also for most
of their radioactivity. Yet these separations were of
a most peculiar nature—they never appeared to be
permanent. The concentrated emanating substance
gradually lost its potency as a source of emanation, and,
more surprising still, the original thorium preparation
slowly regained its lost power to emanate. Clearly, a
very complex situation was revealed by these researches.
With the vision of genius, however, Rutherford went
straight to the root of the matter, ignoring inessentials.
In the first paper of Rutherford and Soddy, what
proved to be the correct view regarding the separable
emanating substance is already maintained: [1]

" . . . the manner in which it makes its appearance
. . . dragged down by precipitates when no question
of insolubility is involved . . . suggests the view
that it is really present in minute quantity. Even
. . . the most active preparations . . . probably are
. . . associated with accidental admixtures probably large in proportion."

[1] *Trans. Chem. Soc.*, April, 1902.

It was in this belief that Rutherford set about obtaining a supply of the purest thorium nitrate possibly obtainable, so that the emanating substance might be studied apart from these accidental impurities which had nothing at all to do with the radioactivity of the specimen. He wrote to Sir William Crookes, in London, telling him of the progress of his researches, and asking him to forward to Knöfler in Germany a request for the very pure materials required.   Crookes was both physicist and chemist, of international repute, and a year or so previously he, too, had separated, from uranium compounds in his case, a highly active constituent responsible for most of the activity.   But he had not followed the matter farther.   In his reply to Rutherford he wrote,[1]

> " M. Becquerel told me a curious circumstance a short time ago, and asked if I could verify it.   He prepared some time ago an inactive uranium nitrate. Now, on repeating his experiment with the identical sample he found it had reassumed its radioactivity. I am at work on old compounds of my own to see if I can get similar results."

Here, evidently, in the work of Crookes and Becquerel, was a parallel case with the thorium one, except that there was no emanation, only the inherent radioactivity, associated with the materials concerned.

When the pure thorium nitrate arrived from Germany Rutherford and Soddy were not long in confirming and extending their original results.   Here, their own words probably afford the briefest and, at the same time, the clearest account of what they found out:[2]

> " The major part of the radioactivity of thorium . . . is due to a non-thorium type of matter, ThX,

[1] 18th December, 1901.   [2] *Trans. Chem. Soc.*, July, 1902.

possessing distinct chemical properties, which is temporarily radioactive. . . . The constant radioactivity of thorium is maintained by the production of this material at a constant rate. . . . The ThX is undergoing a further change, and one of its products is . . . the emanation produced by thorium compounds. The ThX further possesses the property of exciting radioactivity on surrounding inactive matter. . . . Considerations make it probable that it is the same as the excited radioactivity produced by the thorium emanation, which has been shown to be produced by ThX. . . . Thorium can be freed . . . from both ThX and the excited radioactivity . . . and then possesses an activity about 25 per cent of its original value, below which it has not been reduced."

Only one important result is not included in this statement of conclusions. For the ThX (thorium X), the decay both of temporary radioactivity and of emanating power was examined and found to follow a " geometrical progression with the time ", as previously established for the emanation itself (p. 70) and the excited radioactivity (p. 73)—and the recovery of these properties by the original preparation of thorium was found to be exactly complementary to this decay. The half-value period was again different, however, being roughly four days for the ThX.

At this stage, with so many examples of the " geometrical " law established in cases of temporary radioactivity, any attempt to theorize obviously needed no further excuse. Yet, in spite of this, an acceptable theory was not easily to be put forward in a subject so completely new and strange. For, at several points, the situation was still relatively obscure. For example, two novel properties had been predicated—the property of radioactivity, or of emitting ionizing radiations, and the property of producing new kinds of matter. It was not clear how these were connected. Then there were the temporarily radioactive bodies, and those which appeared to be permanently radioactive; it was hardly obvious whether this was a difference merely in degree, or in kind. And, finally, there was a question which placed the whole subject under suspicion with some who had no direct part in its development—whether the suggestion of permanently radioactive substances was not a direct violation of the most cherished of all scientific principles, the principle of energy conservation. There can be little wonder, then, that we can trace the finally successful theory of Rutherford and Soddy through a number of stages of evolution before it emerged in the simplicity of scientific beauty—and acceptability (or truth!). It will probably best serve our present purpose if we examine the theory first in its final simple form, before reversing the order of evolution to discover —what, from the point of view of the history of science, is almost equally important—the earlier and more complicated variants through which it passed.

What was effectively the final form of the theory was given in a paper entitled " Radioactive Change " published in the *Philosophical Magazine* in May, 1903. This paper should be read as a whole if its full significance is to be grasped, for none of it is redundant. However, some idea of the theory, and some light on the obscurities which we have mentioned, may be obtained by even brief quotation. Thus the following statements are pertinent:

" it is not possible to regard radioactivity as a consequence of changes that have already taken place. The rays emitted must be an accompaniment of the change. . . ."

" In all cases where one of the radioactive products has been separated and its activity examined independently of the active substance which gives rise to it, or which it in turn produces . . . the law of radioactive change . . . may be expressed in the one statement—the proportional amount of radioactive matter that changes in unit time is a constant . . . . the constant . . . possesses for each type of active matter a fixed and characteristic value. The complexity of the phenomena of radioactivity is due to the existence as a general rule of several different types of matter changing at the same time into one another, each type possessing a different radioactive constant."

". . . Apparent constancy [of radioactivity] is merely the expression of the slow rate of change of the radioelement. . . . Over sufficiently long periods its radioactivity must also decay according to the law of radioactive change, for otherwise it would be necessary to look upon radioactive change as involving the creation of matter . . . the energy liberated in radioactive processes does not disobey the law of the conservation of energy."

" The law of radioactive change, that the rate of change is proportional to the quantity of changing substance, is also the law of monomolecular chemical reaction. Radioactive change, therefore, must be of such a kind as to involve one system only . . . the changing system must be the chemical atom . . . in radioactive change the chemical atom must suffer disintegration."

The inescapable logic of the whole argument leads up to the sensational conclusion which is the last phrase of our quotation: radioactivity is spontaneous atomic disintegration. The kind of thing that the alchemists had been trying to do for many hundreds of years, Rutherford and Soddy realized, was continually happening in nature without the intervention of human agency: one kind of matter was changing into another, with the gratuitous emission of energy in the form of ionizing radiations.

This revolutionary conclusion was not reached in a single step, nor finally championed without much searching of heart. In published papers its statement slowly became more definite with the passage of months. "The idea of the chemical atom in certain cases spontaneously breaking up with the evolution of energy is not of itself contrary to anything that is known . . .",[1] became " these changes must be occurring within the atom, and the radioactive elements must be undergoing spontaneous transformation ",[2] before crystallizing into the form of our earlier quotation in May, 1903. In less formal ways, in letters to friends and in lectures at McGill, the idea was tried out in order that it should be refined by the test of criticism. After the McGill lectures, at any rate, this criticism was not always dispassionate; fear that disrepute might attach to the university, if one of her young professors began propagating views concerning the instability of material atoms, sometimes brought adversaries into the field who had no title to criticize, but Cox, the senior professor of physics, was a staunch friend and supporter of the new views, and Rutherford

---

[1] *Trans. Chem. Soc.*, July, 1902.

[2] *Phil. Mag.*, September, 1902.

was not unduly influenced by these rebuffs. He wrote to Thomson, and received an encouraging reply:[1]

" . . . it seems to me that your explanation clears up a great deal of obscurity. I am glad it came before the chapter on Radioactivity in my book was printed off. I shall be able to introduce it and make the account much more connected."

He wrote to Sir William Crookes concerning the publication of the papers by the Chemical Society: [2]

" Although of course it is not advisable to put the case too bluntly to a chemical society, I believe that in the radioactive elements we have a process of disintegration or transmutation steadily going on which is the source of the energy dissipated in radioactivity. . . . Mr. Soddy and myself would both be obliged if you could do anything to facilitate the publication of the paper if difficulties arise over ' atomic ' views."

And there is a laconic reply from his friend Zeleny:[3]

" That . . . no doubt shows that something is going on in the way of a transformation."

After the May, 1903, paper was published there were still some dissentients, but, in spite of them, the disintegration theory was " on a flood-tide of interest ", as Soddy had said. In June two important lectures were given in England which bear closely on the point we are considering. On 12th June, Lodge gave the Romanes lecture in the Sheldonian Theatre at Oxford. He spent the second half of the lecture dealing with Rutherford's recent discoveries and theories. He said:

[1] 13th May, 1902.   [2] 29th April, 1902.
[3] 6th June, 1902.

" Plainly if an elementary form of matter is found to
be throwing off another substance . . . here is a fact,
if fact it be, of prodigious importance. . . . Assuming the truth of this strange string of laboratory facts,
we appear to be face to face with a phenomenon
quite new in the history of the world."

Then, a week later, Pierre Curie lectured before the
Royal Institution on " Radium ". It is evident that
his own outlook on the subject, at that stage, had not
advanced far enough for the new theory to be part of
it. For it was never mentioned throughout the whole
of his discourse. Considerable caution was expressed,
even, concerning the truly gaseous nature of the emanations. " The foregoing experiments lead me to picture
the emanation as a gas similar to an ordinary (material)
gas," he said. " However, the hypothesis of the existence of such a gas at present rests solely on radioactive
evidence. Moreover, contrary to what happens with
ordinary matter, the emanation disappears spontaneously when enclosed in a sealed tube." [1] The hint of
suspicion, here, regarding " purely radioactive evidence "
for the existence of matter, is to be contrasted with
Rutherford's wholehearted acceptance of that evidence:

" These various new bodies differ from ordinary
matter, therefore, only in one point, namely, that
their quantity is far below the limit that can be reached
by the ordinary methods of chemical and spectro-
scopic analysis . . . this is no argument against their
specific material existence. . . ." [2]

It requires physical insight, certainly, to base a whole
science on the behaviour of invisible and imponderable

[1] Translated from the original French.
[2] *Phil. Mag.*, May, 1903.

amounts of material, but Rutherford was sufficient of a
realist—and sufficiently conservative in his outlook—
to recognize that the break with traditional physics
was much less drastic according to his way of explaining
the phenomena than according to any other that was
offered.

Yet "explaining", always a dangerous word in
physical science, is probably more than ever extravagant
in this context. Even the process conventionally accepted
as explanation in science—the linking up to something
closer to everyday experience—remained strangely
absent, in respect of the fundamental law of radioactive
change, for at least twenty-five years after this date.
But mere orderly description was an enormous advance;
it was a great achievement to come to the sure realization, from exhaustive experiments, that " the complexity
of the phenomena . . . is due to the existence . . . of
several different types of matter changing at the same
time ". Here, too, the intermediate steps had been
cautious—from the first formal relation in the paper
on the emanation (p. 70), through some inelegant
mathematics enshrining, nevertheless, a clear physical
idea, to be found in a communication bearing the names
of Rutherford and Miss Brooks,[1] to our original quotation. But even that quotation stopped surprisingly
short of the final step in formal description. It fixed
upon the radioactive constant as the important numerical
datum characterizing each radioactive element, but
it certainly did not take the last step of pointing out
that the same quantity that was " the proportional
amount of radioactive matter that changes in unit
time," was obviously, on the disintegration hypothesis,
also an *atomic* constant of clear significance—the prob-

[1] *Phil. Mag.*, July, 1902.

ability (per unit time) that any atom should disintegrate. If this step had been taken, then all the atoms of a given kind of radioactive matter would have been seen to be characterized by the same definite probability of breaking up in any specified short interval of time—and they would have been seen to differ from all the atoms of any other kind of active matter, themselves characterized by a different, but again a constant, disintegration probability. This realization became general only in later years. In 1904 it was still sufficiently incomplete for Soddy, even, to write, in a single context,[1]

" A relation perhaps more generally useful than the radioactive constant is its reciprocal $1/\lambda$ which has a very interesting physical significance. It represents the average life of the metabalon [radioactive atom] in seconds. . . . The average life of a metabalon may be compared with the atomic weight in the case of a stable atom as a constant well suited for its experimental identification. It may be pointed out that the actual life of the different atoms of the same unstable element has all values between zero and infinity. . . . This constitutes the first difference in properties between the individual atoms of the same element that has ever been discovered."

and, in the same publication,

" Radioactivity is a property contributed by a few atoms only in any given instant. . . . For many purposes, however, a property which is contributed by a *constant* fraction of the total is indistinguishable from a property possessed by each atom in common."

In the same week in which the paper " Radioactive

[1] Wilde lecture, Manchester Lit. Phil. Soc., 23rd February, 1904.

Change " was published, Ernest Rutherford, Macdonald professor of physics at McGill University, Montreal, was recommended by the Council of the Royal Society of London for election as fellow. He had been a candidate in the previous year, and according to one of his sponsors had been unlucky not to be elected at his first opportunity. " I am exceedingly surprised and vexed that you were not elected to the Royal Society," this friend wrote on 2nd May, 1902, " every one I spoke with regarded your election as certain." However, as if to make some sort of amends, within a year of his election the Society decided to invite Rutherford to deliver the important Bakerian lecture, and, before another year had elapsed, had conferred on him the added distinction of the Rumford medal. As events proved, these were merely the rumblings before an avalanche of further honours, but in chronicling them thus briefly, even, we have omitted to record certain other facts which should not be overlooked. For, between his recommendation for election as F.R.S. in May, 1903, and his award of the Rumford medal in the November of the following year, Rutherford had twice visited England, and had created an enormous impression by his lectures and his contacts with all sorts of people in many walks of life. Before the first of these visits was half over, Zeleny wrote,[1] " Congratulations . . . [on] the way you have had scientific London at your feet." Even scientific America, it seems, knew that something out of the ordinary was happening on the other side of the Atlantic—and there were those in England, too, who had had a very good idea just what was bound to happen, if Rutherford was given the opportunity. Larmor, the recently appointed secretary

[1] 16th July, 1903.

The time apparatus could not only be used for determination of times of rise of currents in various circuits but also for determining the duration of the current at make or break of the primary circuit.

The method is a very simple one & the duration of the secondary may be determined under whatever conditions we please, since the galvanometer is not connected in series with the secondary but only as a shunt off the secondary.

The battery is connected to the binding screw A & when the lever is in position the current passes from A to B. & then through the primary circuit P, through a resistance box R to the other terminal of the battery.

When the lever is knocked aside the primary current is broken.

The secondary current is connected through a resistance box R_1, & the shunt lever CD

The ballistic galvanometer is a shunt off the lever ED.

Page from Rutherford's dissertation "On Magnetic Viscosity," written in 1895 (see page 30)

Dec 5. 1893

Experiments on secondary currents

After reading Lord Kelvin's article on
[an incidental] illustration of a [shallowing] transient current in
an iron a? . Page 473 Voll III of his collected
works + Lord Raleigh's Article on the
Philosophical magazine for 1886 on [Kelvin]
of conductors conveying alternating current it
occurred to me that Faraday's statement
of the absolute equality of the time integral
[M] of the induced current on making + break
[the] circuit that this was only true in
the case of any [fine] ones or that [to thicker]
of the [more] in the secondary current would [be]
the effect of making the current at make
and break different since the apparent
resistance of conductors increases with the
[rate] [shortness] duration of a transient cur
It was not [observed] till later that
the same [for] idea had occurred to
Sir J. Thompson [rather] in a paper which he
read [before] in [Philosophical magazine] for March
1893 entitled ' On the time integral of a
[transient] electromagnetically [induced cur]

Account of what was probably Rutherford's earliest
piece of post-graduate research, dated 5th December
1893 (*see page 27*)

Since it is well known that iron wire on account of its large permeability exhibits the effect of increased resistance very strongly an iron wire .25 centimetres in diameter & 120 ft long was used.

The & Commutated magnet of an induction coil was wound with a primary & secondary.

The secondary was closed through a the iron wire & a non inductive resistance of 1 ohm

The galvanometer was used as a shunt off the terminals of the 1 ohm resistance. & the current was made and broken by a suitable commutator. It was thought that the deflection of DF would be widely different for the make & break on account of the variation of resistance due to the current circulating in the skin of the iron wire CD. No such effect however could be observed. The result Faraday's result we now know to absolutely true theoretically as demonstrated by Sir William Thomson in his footnote to his article 'on the time Integral of a transient electricity induced current'. March 1840 Philosoph Magazine:

$$f = \frac{2 \cdot h^2 \cdot QR}{SP^2 \cdot QT^2} = \frac{2h^2}{SP^2} \cdot \frac{QR}{Pv} \cdot \frac{Pv}{PV} \cdot \frac{PV}{QV^2} \cdot \frac{QV^2}{QT^2}$$

$$= \frac{2h^2}{SP^2} \cdot \frac{PE}{CP} \cdot \frac{CP^2}{CP \cdot PV \cdot CD^2} \cdot \frac{CD^2}{CB^2}$$

$$\therefore f = \frac{h^2}{SP^2} \cdot \frac{PE}{BC^2} = \frac{h^2}{2SP^2}$$

SECTION III.

ON THE MOTION OF BODIES IN CONIC SECTIONS, UNDER THE ACTION OF FORCES TENDING TO A FOCUS.

PROP. XI. PROBLEM VI.

A body is revolving in an ellipse, to find the law of force tending to a focus of the ellipse.

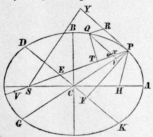

Let S be the focus to which the force tends, P the position of the body at any time, PCG, DCK conjugate diameters, Q a point near P, QT, PF perpendiculars on SP, DCK, from Q, P respectively, PR a tangent at P, QR parallel to SP, Qxv parallel to PR, meeting SP in x, and PC in v, and let SP, DCK intersect in E.

Then $F = \dfrac{2h^2}{SP^2} \cdot \dfrac{QR}{QT^2}$, ultimately, when PQ is indefinitely diminished.

But, by similar triangles QTx, PFE,

$$\frac{QT^2}{Qx^2} = \frac{PF^2}{PE^2} = \frac{PF^2}{AC^2} = \frac{BC^2}{CD^2}.$$

Now, $\dfrac{Qv^2}{Pv.vG} = \dfrac{CD^2}{CP^2}$, by the properties of the ellipse,

It is clear from these expts that chemical nitrogen gives long range of particles which produce scintillations at least as bright as H. & have about the same range (to be tested accurately)

N^2 = .64 for pure N for length 3 cms
No .51 for air p 29 } .47
   .42 -- -- p 42 }

N° to be expected if due to N alone in air = $\frac{4}{5} \times .64$ = .51 in good agreement with that number.

Since introd of CO_2 gives very small effect, it is clear that the no of these particles come from C or O_2 "unimportant"

To settle whether these scintillations are N, He, H or 2He?

Long-range particles from Nitrogen: Rutherford's conclusions as recorded in his laboratory notebook, 9th November, 1917 (*see page 151*)

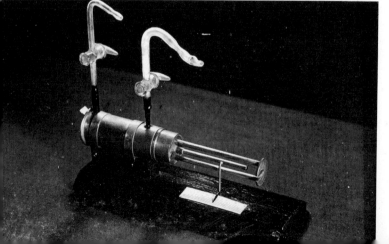

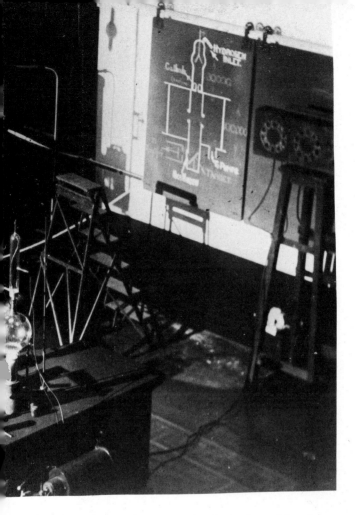

Artificial disintegration by accelerated particles shown as a lecture experiment at the Royal Institution, 1934 (*above*)

Apparatus used by Rutherford and Chadwick, 1921, in researches on the disintegration of certain light elements by α particles, 1921 (*left*)

Discussing the day's results: Rutherford with two
research students at the Cavendish Laboratory, 1936

of the Royal Society, had written to him before he left
Montreal: [1]

"I am glad to hear that you are coming in May:
you may be the lion of the season, for the newspapers
have suddenly become radioactive."

The prediction, certainly, was not very wide of the
mark.

During his absence from Canada in the summer of
1903, Rutherford spent some time in travel in France
and Switzerland—and some time attempting to take a
holiday, in spite of the weather, in North Wales—but
he had with him, most of the time, a large amount of
writing, in the form of the manuscript of his projected
book, which kept him fully occupied. He had been at
work on this for about six months before he left, and he
was making a brave attempt to get it into final form,
with all the latest experimental results interpreted in
terms of the disintegration theory, during his long vacation. He had agreed to publish the book in the Cambridge Physical Series and was eager to get it finished.
But other things intervened, and work on the book
dragged on until the end of the year.

One of the things which intervened was the meeting
of the British Association at Southport in the first week
in September. It had been arranged that Rutherford
should open a discussion on the nature of the emanations
from radium at this meeting, immediately following
the delivery of the formal address by the sectional president. Normally, Rutherford would have been encouraged
rather than daunted by this prospect of a popular
audience, for his disintegration theory had already

[1] 3rd April, 1903.

been widely accepted, but a new situation was created by an action of Lord Kelvin. At 79—and four years retired from his Glasgow professorship—Kelvin was almost a legendary, but still a very influential, figure in British science. Any lead from him, therefore, was bound to command serious attention, whatever the subject. On this occasion he had arranged for the printing and circulation to members of the association, before the meeting, of a communication on the subjects covered by Rutherford's address, but decidedly critical of the views that Rutherford was known to hold. No doubt the communication was hardly more than the act of rebellion of an old man against the new ideas— and its terms were in no sense dogmatic (" I shall look forward with eagerness to the earliest published reports of the discussion," the statement maintained, for Kelvin was unable to be present in person), but the very exist-tence of the pamphlet was itself unsettling for the lec-turer. Rutherford, though he had been acclaimed and fêted, was still young; at the age of thirty-two he was somewhat apprehensive of the outcome of this en-counter with the doyen of physicists. He appealed to his scientific friends to support him in the discussion, if need arose. In the actual event, however, his worst fears proved groundless, and this support of mere numbers was never required.

Rutherford returned to Canada immediately the meeting at Southport came to an end, and was soon plunged into experimental work again. But now he began to be bombarded—and it is true to say that the bombardment hardly ceased throughout the rest of his life, whether in North America or in England— with requests for lectures: to the public, to university audiences, and at seemingly innumerable congresses.

One of the first of these requests was on behalf of the American Association for the Advancement of Science, which was holding its " convocation week " at St. Louis over the New Year. The permanent secretary wrote: [1]

" It has been the custom for a number of years . . . [to have] at least one public lecture complimentary to the citizens of the city which is entertaining the Association, and this year, since radium seems to be the principal scientific topic of the day, it has seemed rather appropriate to arrange if possible for such a lecture on the subject of radium."

Rutherford agreed to deliver the lecture and made the journey of 1250 miles each way by rail for the sole purpose of its delivery. Probably hearing of this exploit, Sir Oliver Lodge wrote: [2]

" I trust you will not waste your time in lecturing but will go on with your experiments and leave the lecturing to others."

To a large extent, no doubt, that was Rutherford's view, too, but the same mail that brought Lodge's note of advice also brought the first inquiry from the secretary of the Royal Society, regarding the possibility that Rutherford would be able to make his second journey to England within twelve months, to deliver the Bakerian lecture—usually fixed for a date early in March. Again, the occasion was sufficiently important to prompt acceptance, although in the course of correspondence the traditional date was eventually abandoned in favour of Thursday, 19th May. When news

[1] 4th November, 1903.   [2] 4th January, 1904.

of the lecture became known, other invitations quickly followed. In this way a Royal Institution discourse on Friday, 20th May, was fixed up in Rutherford's name.

Rutherford arrived in England during the first week in May, about a fortnight after his book *Radio-activity* had been published by the Cambridge press. This book and his two chief lectures made the visit an unqualified success. It lasted no more than a few weeks, but within that time he was the recipient of unstinted recognition and praise from so many of his seniors as perhaps never before greeted a young experimenter from a distant land. Lord Rayleigh, Sir Norman Lockyer, Sir William Huggins, A. J. Balfour, besides those whose names we already know as supporters of his views—even Kelvin himself—sought the further acquaintance of the young professor. Then, in less than a month he was on the high seas again, on the way back to Montreal—and work. Shortly afterwards, on the question of publicity and work, Rutherford wrote to his mother: [1]

" I am getting as much advertisement as is good for me. These things, however, don't count scientifically, for it is work that tells."

So let us take another last look at a sample of that work, before bringing this chronicle of the Montreal period to an end, with a mere recital of a long list of further honours and notable achievements.

During the years 1901–2, whilst the collaboration with Soddy—already fully described—was leading to such outstanding results, Rutherford was also engaged on other experiments of first-rate importance, both in

[1] 10th August, 1904.

conjunction with students and by himself. If this extra work is to be set alongside the output of the Rutherford-Soddy combination in the same two years (p. 78), then, in sheer weight of printer's ink, another eighty-seven pages of text, divided amongst five published papers, are to be recorded. The paper with Miss Brooks, which has already been mentioned (p. 90), was one of the five; now two others assume greater importance for immediate discussion. They are two papers describing the results of detailed experiments into the nature of the radiations from radioactive substances. One represents collaboration with A. G. Grier, the other is by Rutherford himself, and both papers furnish information which was of great importance in the development of the disintegration theory during the years under review. The two questions—concerning the sequence of radioactive transformation products, and the radiations which are emitted in the course of the changes—are, clearly, complementary aspects of the single problem of atomic disintegration, which so far we have treated in the first aspect, only. We have, hitherto, carefully avoided the second aspect of the problem for the sake of some clarity of presentation, but we cannot—and we should not—avoid this aspect indefinitely. So we return at once to the question which until now has been shelved—and to the two papers which deal with it.

The first paper, that describing the work with Grier, concerns the more penetrating or β-radiation, Rutherford's own contribution has to do with the less penetrating or α-radiation; the first paper is to some extent confirmatory of earlier results, the second is more important in that it reaches entirely new conclusions. Before these two papers were published, the general consensus of opinion was that the β-rays were to be identified with streams of negative electrons projected from the active matter, while the α-rays were a type of easily absorbed Röntgen radiation. This, for example, was categorically stated in an article by Thomson in *Harper's Magazine* only a month before the papers appeared.   Afterwards, the former view was substantiated, but the latter was shown to be entirely wrong: the α-rays were proved by Rutherford, by the most careful and conclusive experiments, to be positively charged particles, thousands of times heavier than electrons—atomic fragments comparable in mass with the lightest atoms, those of hydrogen and helium— projected in the act of disintegration with velocities of the order of $\frac{1}{20}$ to $\frac{1}{15}$ of the velocity of light.   This was a result of enormous importance; until it was established there were many who could never follow the lead of Rutherford's intuitive genius in regarding the α-radiation as the most important feature for investigation—and many others who found it unnecessary, or at least difficult, to distinguish, as he always insisted that they should, between radioactive "emanations" and "radiations".   Soddy saw the difficulties of these two groups of scientists in clear perspective.   He wrote, in partial apology for those of the first group: [1]

" It is a matter of remark how nearly the corpuscular forms of radiation resemble the undulatory variety as exampled by the X-ray.   It furnishes a remarkable vindication of the insight of Newton into natural phenomena, that, when the process he imagined light to be was discovered three centuries after, it

[1] Wilde lecture, 23rd February, 1904.

should have been first taken for a different variety of light vibration."

—and, in correction of those of the latter: [1]

" [The emanation] gives out rays it is true, but to confuse it with the rays themselves would be to mistake a cannon for a cannon ball."

After this discovery—after Rutherford's proof of the corpuscular nature of the α-radiation—the whole subject of radioactivity took on a new interest. In particular, a result of Pierre Curie and Laborde, announced a month or so previously, appeared differently to Rutherford and those who had accepted his latest conclusions, from what it did to those who had not. Curie and Laborde had discovered a new property of radium preparations — that they are continuously generating heat, so that in any ordinary circumstances the active material is maintained at a temperature appreciably greater than that of its surroundings. Amongst physicists of the old order, chiefly, this announcement caused great consternation, for the subject of heat was one which they thought they understood. Once more it seemed, for the moment, that accepted notions of conservation were called in question by the new discoveries. Rutherford, however, was neither so surprised nor so alarmed. He thought it not unreasonable to suppose that the heat which Curie and Laborde had observed was just the ultimately degraded form of the energy of motion of the α-rays—degraded according to the accepted laws of the most orthodox. When he returned to Montreal after the British Association meeting in September, 1903, this was the piece of

[1] *McGill University Magazine*, 1903.

experimental work to which he immediately devoted all his energies—a further investigation of the process of generation of heat in radium preparations.

He at once entered into collaboration with one of the senior members of the McGill staff, Professor H. T. Barnes. It was a happy circumstance that such collaboration was possible: in H. L. Callendar's time at McGill the accurate measurement of quantities of heat was one of the problems to which the chief resources of the laboratory were directed—and Barnes was Callendar's assistant in all this work. He was able from the first, therefore, to bring to the new problem a long experience of the sort of measurement required. In October, a short preliminary account of the work was sent off for publication in *Nature*, and by the end of December a full-length paper was ready for communication to the editors of the *Philosophical Magazine*. Rutherford and Barnes had proved, beyond all possible doubt, that the evolution of heat was directly connected with the emission of α-particles, and they had followed in some detail the contribution to the total effect of the α-particles emitted by the emanation and the active deposit (excited radioactivity), as well as the residual effect of the α-particles from radium itself. As regards actual quantities, they had closely confirmed the figures of Curie and Laborde: pure radium generates heat in this way in amount sufficient to raise the temperature of its own weight of water from freezing to boiling-point each hour, supposing no loss of heat occurs and the radium is accompanied by its products of disintegration. The heat, then, represents the original energy of the α-particles—and Rutherford and Barnes were not slow to point out, on the basis of simple arithmetical calculation, that the comparatively enormous amount which is involved indicates immediately that the α-particles must obtain their energy from some unsuspected store of energy somehow available in the atoms of radioactive matter, but not so available in atoms of stable matter. Once more, therefore, for his conclusions did not admit of disbelief, Rutherford made the essential contribution, as regards experimentation and interpretative advance, in a branch of his subject in which, for a time, it seemed that others would precede him.

Amongst the events of 1904, the publication of *Radioactivity* has already been briefly referred to; it was such an important event for modern physics that it should not be left without further comment. At the time in question a review of the whole subject was urgently needed, for it had become extremely complicated. Yet a mere review was hardly enough; a unifying theory was required, if the scattered data were to be brought into reasonable compass, and into a satisfactory relation one with another. In collaboration with Soddy, Rutherford had just developed such a theory; he was the obvious man to make a success of the undertaking. If it is needed, to confirm the impression which may still be obtained on reading his book, there is abundant testimony from contemporary letters to show that success was immediate. Thus, W. C. D. Whetham (now Sir William Dampier), the editor of the Cambridge Physical Series who dealt with the book, wrote, as soon as he had passed the last batch of proofs for the printers:[1]

" It has been a great pleasure to me to help your book through the Press, and I have learned much during the process."

[1] 17th March, 1904.

Then, there was an American acquaintance who was so sure that, in later days, the book would come to be considered epoch-making that he bargained to receive the first copy that was issued—and Rutherford took him seriously! He inquired of the publishers if there was any sense in which " first copy " could properly be understood, and he afterwards kept to his bargain and sent this acquaintance the first of the six author's copies which he himself received on the day of publication for private distribution. The American soon replied with a compliment:[1]

> ". . . allow me to thank you for your thoughtfulness and courtesy in sending me copy No. 1 of your wonderful classic."

Finally, there was a long eulogy which must have pleased Rutherford more than most of the rest. It came from H. A. Bumstead of Yale. Rutherford and Bumstead met first in New York in 1902, when Kelvin was lecturing there, and the two men quickly discovered many interests in common. Afterwards, Bumstead wrote:[2]

> " I have become slightly radioactive since the very pleasant evening which I spent in your company. . . yet it is only excited activity at best."

Then, nearly eighteen months later:[3]

> " I got hold of your new book yesterday and have read most of it, last night and this morning. I want to offer you my warm congratulations on the admirable clearness of the language, the good arrangement and the great logical force of your presentation of

[1] G. F. Kunz, 2nd June, 1904.   [2] 4th January, 1903.
[3] 5th June, 1904.

the theory . . . unless I am prejudiced, the future historian of physics is going to think a lot of this book as a most brilliant example of the application of the true scientific method to a perplexing problem. It is going to be one of the classics."

To choose a lighter vein, the publication of *Radio-activity* also brought Rutherford a letter from a Scots padre who had been a fellow-traveller—and whist-player— on the journey from New Zealand in 1895. Nine years later, seeing a notice of the new book in his local news-paper, he wrote from his Glasgow parish:[1]

" Our acquaintance was not a long one but it was long enough to give me the feeling that S.S. *Mariposa* had been fortunate in shipping a fair quantity of brains at Auckland, and it is always pleasing because flattering to a man to have his impressions and judgments amply confirmed."

And this brings us to Rutherford's own estimate of the success of his book. In the introductory section he wrote:

" The value of any working theory depends upon the number of experimental facts it serves to correlate, and upon its power of suggesting new lines of work. In these respects the disintegration theory, whether or not it may ultimately be proved correct, has already been justified by its results."

It need only be added to this modest evaluation, that thirty-five more years of intensive research in the subject which he developed have merely increased the evidence in favour of the correctness of Rutherford's theory— which throughout the whole of that time has been

[1] 3rd May, 1904.

prolific beyond measure in " suggesting new lines of work ".

Rutherford was three years more at McGill after the publication of *Radio-activity*. In respect of experiments these were years of thorough consolidation rather than sensational advance; as regards personal reputation they were years of well-sustained triumph. Keen young men joined themselves to his laboratory: H. L. Bronson from Yale, T. Godlewski from Lemberg, Otto Hahn, a young German chemist who had followed Soddy in Ramsay's laboratory at University College, London, and M. Levin, after he had taken his doctorate at Göttingen. A. S. Eve, recently appointed to the mathematics staff at McGill, wandered over into the neighbouring department and became a permanency there: evidently seventeen years as assistant master at Marlborough College had not lessened his enthusiasm for fundamental research. And, last of all, Miss Brooks and R. K. McClung, both of whom had been in the laboratory in former days, returned after spending some time working in the Cavendish Laboratory at Cambridge. All of these were provided with thoroughly worth-while problems: some of them made discoveries of great importance under Rutherford's guidance. Thus Hahn, who had already concluded that there must be at least one transformation product intermediate between thorium and thorium X in the disintegration series, whilst working in London, when he came to Montreal quickly substantiated this discovery and added another. And Eve, amongst other results, soon amassed a deal of evidence to show that there was, after all, a type of radiation from radioactive materials of the type of Röntgen or X-radiation—not the least penetrating component, as originally thought, but, instead, the most penetrating—the component discovered by Villard in 1900, which has not so far been mentioned in this account, and which its discoverer referred to as γ-radiation. Hahn returned to Berlin after about a year, and in rapid succession a number of new active products were announced as the result of his researches. Eve remained at McGill, and in due course found himself in the position which Rutherford had occupied, as Macdonald professor.

At this stage it is interesting to refer to Sir William Macdonald's own reaction to the altogether unexampled success which, within a few years, had rewarded the bold policy of appointing, to one of the chairs which he financed, a young man of twenty-seven. In July, 1901, he agreed to increase the endowment of the chair substantially, and in the following year he provided the money for the purchase of a machine for the production of liquid air for the physics department—and three hundred dollars in order that Rutherford should be able to buy some pure radium bromide, not long before raised to the class of a marketable commodity through the labours of the German chemist, Giesel. Then, a little later still, when the award of the Rumford medal had been announced (p. 92), and the members of the physics department were beginning to discuss plans for a dinner to commemorate the occasion, Sir William took affairs into his own hands, " declared he would finance the whole dinner and left them to ask any number they liked. He declared that it was his physics building and his Professor and he was going to do the thing in style." [1] So, at the Windsor Hotel, on 7th December, 1904, the Principal of the university presided over " a very distinguished gathering ", and

[1] Rutherford to his mother, 4th December, 1904.

a toast list with seven lengthy speeches kept the diners in their seats until well after midnight.

The award of the Rumford medal has already been spoken of as the beginning of an avalanche of honours, which is no exaggeration: what followed was indeed an avalanche—and many a young man would have been carried away by the force of its impact.   Just returned from a second visit to St. Louis in September, 1904, where he had been chief speaker in the " Physics of the Electron " section of the International Congress of Arts and Science arranged in connexion with the Universal Exposition, Rutherford received a pressing invitation from the President of Yale to deliver the third course of Silliman lectures in the spring of 1905. J. J. Thomson and C. S. Sherrington had been the first two lecturers and, now that the turn of a physical, rather than a biological, subject had come round again, Rutherford was the obvious choice.   He had given an isolated lecture there six months previously, and in the· interim there had been tentative discussions between the authorities and himself regarding the possibility of his accepting a professorship at Yale.   This, no doubt, gave the suggestion greater attractiveness from either side.   Rutherford accepted the invitation, and spent three weeks at New Haven at the end of March and the beginning of April.   It is one of the conditions which attach to the lectureship, that a connected account of the lectures shall afterwards be published in book form;   this duly appeared under the title *Radioactive Transformations*, in September, 1906.   Meanwhile, the first edition of *Radio-activity* had rapidly been exhausted, and a second, much enlarged, edition was produced towards the end of 1905. The preparation of these books for the press must undoubtedly have involved a great amount of hard work, but it is characteristic of Rutherford's entire achievement that this seemed to take its place in the scheme of things, without the results losing value in consequence. Even before the Silliman lectures were delivered, a request came from California that Rutherford should lecture at Berkeley at the summer session of the University of California. But the course of lectures at Yale had been put forward a week or two so that he could leave early for a summer holiday in New Zealand, and all invitations, including that from Berkeley, had to be declined in consequence. Mrs. Rutherford and their daughter Eileen, by this time a child of three years, had already been away from Montreal for seven months, taking advantage of the summer in New Zealand, and Rutherford left to join them, as soon as he was able to make the necessary arrangements, on his return from New Haven.

When the Rutherfords returned to Montreal in the autumn of 1905, the budget of invitations, and reminders of earlier invitations, had increased beyond all hope of satisfaction. To the greater number of these the reply had to be in the sense of that to Dr. S. C. Prescott, secretary of the Society of Arts of the Massachusetts Institute of Technology at Boston:[1]

"I have been steadily hoping to see my way clear through a press of work but the work has rather accumulated than receded. . . . I . . . have not any leisure to even consider outside lectures,"

but there were a few which received more favourable consideration. The renewed invitation from the University of California was accepted, and others from the

[1] 27th February, 1906.

Franklin Institute in Philadelphia and from the University of Illinois were singled out for similar treatment. The occasion at Philadelphia came first in the calendar. On 17th, 18th, and 19th April, 1906, the Franklin Institute was celebrating the bicentenary of the birth of Benjamin Franklin, and Rutherford had been asked to speak on " Modern theories of electricity and their relation to the Franklinian theory ", on the second day of the celebrations.   We have already made use of quotations from this brilliant address in the first chapter of this book (p. 14). Two further extracts at the present stage may serve to show that Rutherford was neither entirely blind to the qualities of his own genius, nor yet dazzled by its achievements. Completely unconnected one from the other in the course of the address, occur the following reflections:

" Without detracting in the least from the merit of these philosophers, it is not unreasonable to suppose that the turbidity of their writings was a fair index of the state of their conceptions."

" We recognize that Franklin possessed unusual clearness of physical insight, but we must refrain for that reason from endowing him with the uncanny gift of prophetic vision."

These are incisive remarks, communicating their meaning directly at the first moment of reading, yet with certain qualities, too, hardly less evident on more mature consideration. The force of Rutherford's writing, both popular and scientific, is not to be found in the utter directness of his logical address, nor in strict adherence to the more exact rules of grammar. The simplicity of his presentation is, in a sense, above logic, unencumbered by minute conformity with the canons of syntax. In later years all the original force of writing remained, yet the logician and the grammarian were to find less and less cause for self-flattery in viewing the result.

Shortly before he left Montreal to attend the Franklin celebrations, Rutherford was informed that the University of Pennsylvania proposed to confer on him the honorary degree LL.D. in the course of the commemoration. This was his first honorary degree, but it did not long remain his only one. On 20th June, on his way to California, he broke his journey at Madison to receive a similar award from the University of Wisconsin. " I am rather youthful for such honours," he wrote to his mother,[1] " as they are usually the special perquisite of septuagenarians."

After these many ways in which scientific men in North America expressed their appreciation of Rutherford and his work have been briefly recounted, there remains but one further type of tribute to be dealt with in order to bring this long catalogue to an end. From time to time, over a period of about five years, he received offers of professorships and executive posts in other institutions which were a constant source of embarrassment to him. " These offers . . . are very gratifying, but they annoy me on account of their unsettling effect," he wrote [2] in respect of one of them —and this was true of them all. The position at University College, London, has already been mentioned (p. 80), and also the beginnings of the attempt of the authorities at Yale to annex Rutherford and find a home for him in the Sloane Physics Laboratory. Between the dates of these two offers, moreover, there

[1] 11th April, 1906.
[2] To his mother, 22nd May, 1905.

had been another, a dignified yet persistent call from
Columbia University in New York, which eventually
was as firmly declined. Then the offer from Yale was
repeated—and it proved to have much to commend it.
There was already a strong school of radioactive research
there, with H. A. Bumstead and B. B. Boltwood as chief
exponents, and financially, too, the offer increased in
attractiveness in the later stages. But in January, 1906,
at long last, that offer also was declined, and about the
same time one from King's College, London, likewise
fell through owing to a change in circumstances beyond
Rutherford's control. In the following October two
further invitations were received and these made no
greater impression than those which had preceded
them. The first was a suggestion that Rutherford should
become secretary of the Smithsonian Institution in
Washington, a " position . . . corresponding more to
that of a Cabinet Secretary than to the secretary of a
corporation or society," as it was represented to him,
the second an inquiry from the physics department of
Stanford University, California, which Rutherford had
visited during his far-western trip. Probably neither
offer had much to commend it as an independent
proposition, but another fact, too, certainly operated to
produce the refusals. About the middle of September
Rutherford received a personal letter from Arthur
Schuster, then professor of physics in the University of
Manchester. Schuster was in his middle fifties and had
held his professorship for nearly twenty years; he was
a man of considerable wealth and wide interests, and
the regular duties of the head of a department were
beginning to conflict with ideas of the things which he
might do if only he had leisure. He confided in Rutherford his intention to retire, and he pressed him to

consider, both seriously and with the minimum delay, whether or not he would care to be nominated his successor. By the beginning of November the position had developed to such a degree that the senate was able to make a definite offer, and in the first week of January, 1907, Rutherford's final acceptance was announced in the press. He would begin his duties with the new academical year, on 1st October, and he would, in fact, arrive in England in the early summer in order to have everything completely settled when the new year began.

As was natural, this announcement brought a flood of messages from both sides of the ocean, the majority of which have no place in this biography. But one or two are worthy of comment. Schuster was so gratified with the success of a scheme which had been entirely of his own planning and which he had consistently furthered, that on 15th January he wrote declaring his intention of endowing " for the next few years a Readership in Mathematical Physics ", hoping that ultimately the university would be induced to take over the project, and finally raise the status of the office to that of a full professorship. We shall hear more of the holders of this readership in the next chapter—and we shall then have a chance of appreciating the foresight of the man who was responsible for bringing their additional strength to Rutherford's aid during his years at Manchester.

From McGill, expressions of regret and good wishes may be typified by a personal letter from the Dean of Applied Science, Dr. H. T. Bovey:[1]

" I cannot say how sorry I am that the blow has at last fallen. . . . I knew that the separation must

[1] 5th January, 1907.

come sooner or later and I cannot but frankly express the opinion that you have made a right decision."

American correspondents echoed similar, and stronger, sentiments—and each in turn begged that Rutherford would go and visit him once more before his departure —before he " became a real Englishman " as one of them [1] expressed the supposed change that was to come.   From England, even before the final announcement was made, Thomson wrote: [2]

" I was very glad to hear from Schuster that there was a chance of your coming to England.   I hope it is true . . . it will be very delightful to have you back again."

So the remaining months rapidly passed.   Rutherford continued working at the laboratory and fulfilled what outside lecture engagements he could manage to place in an overburdened time-table.   He was presented with the honorary degree of Doctor of Laws of McGill at a convocation in the last week in April, and, on the morning of 17th May, he took train at Montreal for the boat—and England.   At the station a crowd of friends had gathered to say farewell; later in the same day one of them wrote to him [3] his first letter from Canada:

" I am writing you this feeling exceedingly lonely. The time of parting came at last as it always does . . . and now I return to this building that is associated in every corner with you and your splendid work and with the most delightful memories of my relations with you."

[1] Bumstead, 28th February, 1907.   [2] 18th December, 1906.
[3] H. T. Barnes.

Rutherford was not thirty-six years old; he was a few months younger than Carnot and Hertz, and not many older than Roger Cotes had been, when early death robbed science of the further labours of great men. Lasting fame crowned the achievements of their brief lives; yet upon Rutherford's work, up to this stage, alone, rests an even surer claim to posterity's regard.

CHAPTER 5

Manchester, 1907-1919

IN the last chapter we have discussed, occasionally in considerable detail, Rutherford's work and thought during the period of less than nine years which elapsed between his leaving Cambridge and his return to England in the early summer of 1907. As the title of the present chapter indicates, this period at Montreal was followed by one of twelve years in which he held the Manchester professorship—first through seven years of peace for England, then through five years of war, and the immediate aftermath of war. In his own subject, Rutherford's achievement in these two periods was remarkably similar in many particulars; each saw a great output of work steadily mounting to a stupendous total, each witnessed the putting forward of at least one theory of fundamental importance, revolutionizing current conceptions and pointing the way to vast new fields for research. That there will ever be complete agreement as to which period was the greater, in any ultimate analysis, is extremely unlikely. Yet in this book, at least, these two periods must be treated each on a very different basis, and lest this—and the disproportion in allotted space which results from this treatment—be taken as the expression of a strong conviction on one side rather than the other, it will be well for the difference in treatment to be explained at the outset.

In dealing with Rutherford at Montreal it has been necessary to build up for the reader a complete framework of physical ideas, for without such a framework the entire work and its implications could not usefully have been discussed. This has necessitated frequent digressions and—apart from them—a closer adherence to the historical sequence of actual experimental research than might otherwise have been useful. Now, in dealing with Rutherford at Manchester, the physical ideas may be taken for granted; little need be added to them except when new modifications of outlook occur as the story proceeds. And, in respect of order, there are two reasons, perhaps, why a chronological sequence is no longer expedient. In the first place, the mere volume of work done makes any attempt at completeness of treatment impossible: in Manchester Rutherford became the leader of a large school of active research workers, whilst previously he had been much more alone—an outstanding experimenter with a small band of very capable helpers. And, secondly, as the subject advanced, after the first year or two at Manchester, problems of a more recondite nature began to be studied. These were all-important in their place, but, in a popular account, justice cannot be done to their great significance. It must suffice, therefore, that attention is confined, for the future, to the wider issues, and that details are left for the specialist to discover for himself.

It has been recorded that Rutherford left Montreal on 17th May, 1907. On 6th June in the same year— less than three weeks later—he set up an emanation electroscope in his new laboratory at Manchester and resumed the experiments on which he had last been engaged. Then, presumably, he began to look around him—at the laboratory, and his assistants. The laboratory was newer than the one which he had left at McGill, but not so elaborate; on the other hand his assistants were very much more numerous. Then, apart from pure physics, in the same building, for the time being, sub-departments of electro-chemistry and electro-technology had their only accommodation. For these departments, Rutherford, as professor of physics, was ultimately responsible; their personnel and appliances, therefore, offered additional possibilities for collaboration in exceptional cases. For Rutherford, to possess such possibilities was always attractive; he saw how to use them more readily than did the ordinary person. Thus, when he arrived in the laboratory, certain experiments were in progress on the development of pressure in the explosion of cordite; he had not been there a month before J. E. Petavel,[1] who was conducting the experiments, was prevailed upon to introduce a small quantity of radium emanation into his bomb before making the explosion, whilst Rutherford followed the radioactivity at a distance, utilizing the ionizing action of the γ-rays which escaped through the steel walls of the bomb as a measure of that activity. Previously all the rigours of intense cold and great heat had entirely failed to have any effect on the processes of radioactive disintegration; Rutherford was not going to miss the opportunity of testing in the simplest possible manner whether subjection to high pressures was equally ineffective. Pressures of 1200 atmospheres were attained in the tests, but no certain change in the rate of radioactive decay was established.

However, this was quite a subsidiary investigation; it was spectacular, it provided an entertaining subject

[1] Afterwards Sir Joseph Petavel, director of the National Physical Laboratory.

for a minor paper at the meeting of the British Association at Leicester in August, but nothing more. At this
meeting Rutherford was one of the most sought-out of
speakers. He contributed the opening survey to a
discussion on " The constitution of the atom " which
attracted widespread interest, and, probably for the
first time since he returned to England, he found himself in the midst of a large number of his scientific
friends. " Everybody is very kind and apparently glad
to see me back for good in England," he wrote to his
mother.[1] Then, within a week or two, he had returned
to Manchester again and was ready to begin the year's
work in earnest. There was much to be done; new
courses of lectures to be prepared, and research problems to be arranged for about fifteen students who
were expecting to begin work under his direct supervision. Rutherford wrote down a list of " Researches
possible ", in entirely haphazard order, as it seems,
under two heads, " Radioactive experiments " and
experiments with the " Pressure apparatus ". Under
the first head twenty-four possible experiments are
listed; under the second, six. Numbers (7) and (21)
of the first list are of outstanding importance, they are
described as " Scattering of α-rays " and " Number of
α-rays from radium ", respectively. Practically the
whole of our discussion of Rutherford's output of scientific
work in the Manchester period will centre round these
two experiments, taken, however, as they were in fact
carried out, in the opposite order in time.

We have already seen how Rutherford first came to
the conclusion that the emission of α-radiation from
radioactive substances was really the ejection, in the
course of atomic disintegration, of positively charged

[1] 18th August, 1907.

atoms, probably of hydrogen or helium, with great velocity; the advances we have now to describe followed directly from the experimental realization of methods of detecting such fast-moving atoms individually. Rutherford had long realized that great advances must lie in that direction:

> " I hope you are having good luck with your α-ray counting and that when they are properly enumerated you will feel the need for a little vacation in New Haven,"

Bumstead had written [1] nearly three months before Rutherford left Montreal, but the progress of the attack on the problem had until then been much less rapid than his friend's remark might be taken to imply. Eventually he succeeded, at Manchester, as soon as any of his rivals, in detecting individual particles (from now on we use the term " α-particle ", in the singular, to denote a swiftly-moving charged atom belonging to a beam of " α-rays "), but, in retrospect, his earlier failure is somewhat surprising.   It sprang from the natural, but in this case the shortsighted, conviction that the only hope of solution lay in the attempt to detect the electrical effect, that is the direct ionizing action, of the individual α-particle.   Let us explain the matter further.

Any effect which is to be made the basis of the separate detection of α-particles must rely on the transformation of the energy of motion of the particle into some other kind of energy—electrical, luminous or thermal.   Our problem is to know which type of transformation will give rise to the most easily   observable effect.   First, perhaps, we should   try   to   appreciate   exactly   how

---

[1] 28th February, 1907.

minute is the quantity of mechanical energy available
—for the energy of the α-particle has also been referred
to by other writers, and truly so, as about the *largest*
amount of energy ever found concentrated on a single
atom in nature—before we attempt to weigh these
possibilities. Consider a mechanical system, such as a
bar oscillating at the end of a torsion wire. In any
actual case, if such a system is left to itself, the oscillations gradually die down owing to loss of energy in
frictional processes. Let us take a very small system so
arranged that this loss of energy is exceedingly slow.
Suppose the bar is made of gold about a centimetre
long and weighing one gramme. Suppose it is oscillating
with a period of one second suspended in a vessel so
exhausted of air that it takes five minutes for the oscillation to die down to one half its original amplitude.
Then the amount of mechanical energy lost during each
oscillation, that is in each second of time, when the
motion is already so reduced that the ends of the bar
move only through one half a millimetre from side to
side during the oscillation of the bar, is roughly equal
to the kinetic energy of the fastest α-particle emitted in
radioactive disintegration. We have to try to envisage
the transformation of such a small amount of energy
into electrical, luminous or thermal form, and to imagine the possibilities of registering the ultimate effects.
Rutherford and Soddy had already calculated in 1903 [1]
that it should be possible to do this for the electrical
transformation, and, though they made use of approxi-
mate data and were bold in their assumptions, there
was nothing essentially wrong with their conclusions.
They had themselves been deeply impressed—and
they were beginning to impress the rest of the world—

[1] " Radioactive Change ", *Phil. Mag.*, May, 1903.

with the sensitivity of the electrical method in setting in evidence utterly minute amounts of radioactive matter, and there was every excuse for the extent of this success blinding them—or blinding Rutherford at a somewhat later date—to the claims of another method in relation to the slightly different problem of the detection of individual α-particles. This other method, which might have been developed much earlier than it was, is based upon the transformation of the mechanical energy of the α-particle into luminous energy.

The phosphorescence produced in certain materials by the action of radioactive rays was one of the first effects of the new radiations to be noticed when concentrated preparations of radium were obtained in 1898. Then, in 1903, Crookes made a most notable advance in this branch of the subject—and two German physicists, Elster and Geitel, independently made a similar discovery. Crookes examined a " phosphorescent " screen of zinc sulphide powder under the action of a source of radiation not sufficiently strong to cause a general intense illumination of the screen. With a low-powered microscope he found that the screen presented an ever-changing array of bright points of light, flashing in and out with great rapidity. Very quickly the effect was shown to be due almost entirely to the α-radiation, and the suggestion was soon advanced that each flash of light was caused by the impact of a single α-particle on the screen. Rutherford adopted this suggestion in his first book on radioactivity (1904):

" In the scintillations of zinc sulphide, we are actually witnessing the effect produced by the impact on the screen of single atoms of matter projected with enormous velocity."[1]

[1] p. 128.

—which makes it the more surprising that, for four years afterwards, he allowed himself to be bound by another opinion, which he also expressed in the same book:

> "This . . . would offer a very convenient means of actually counting the number of the particles . . ., if each particle gave rise to a flash of light. It is not likely, however, that this would be the case."[1]

He had occasion to investigate the scintillation effect from time to time during the next few years, but apparently he never gave serious thought to the production of a really efficient screen, in which each particle incident should, almost certainly, give rise to its flash of light.

As we have already mentioned, Rutherford took up the question of the counting of the α-particles again when the laboratory at Manchester was properly organized for his own investigations, but again he persevered with the electrical method of recording. For the purpose of the experiment he took into collaboration Dr. Hans Geiger, Schuster's young assistant, who had already been one year in Manchester when Rutherford arrived.

After a period of many difficulties, the electrical method was made to work in the spring of 1908. A chamber was constructed with a very small aperture, and when α-particles were allowed to pass through this aperture at a sufficiently slow rate, the entry of each was recorded by the sudden movement of a spot of light on a scale, indicating the deflection of a sensitive electrometer. The whole success of the arrangement was due to an ingenious method of first magnifying

[1] p. 129.

considerably the electrical effect of each particle, before attempting its detection. But, in the meanwhile, in Berlin, Regener had also been bringing the scintillation method to a state of efficiency, and had already published his first results and his recipe for success. So Rutherford and Geiger, before completing the experiment with their new arrangement, made a careful comparison of the two methods of detection. They obtained some special screens of phosphorescent zinc sulphide from a first-class dealer, and discovered, no doubt with some surprise, that the electrical and the scintillation counts were almost identical. Two quotations from their subsequent paper [1] will illustrate the position which had thus developed. In the introduction we find:

> " In considering a possible method of counting the number of α-particles, their well-known property of producing scintillations . . . at once suggests itself. . . . No confidence can be placed in such a method of counting the total number of α-particles . . ., until it can be shown that the number so obtained is in agreement with that determined by some other independent method. . . ." [2]

—and, towards the conclusion:

> " The result, however, brings out clearly that within the limit of experimental error, each α-particle produces a scintillation on a properly prepared screen of zinc sulphide. The agreement of the two methods of counting the α-particles is in itself a strong evidence of the accuracy obtained in counting the α-particles . . . by the electrical method. It is now clear that

[1] *Proc. Roy. Soc.*, August, 1908.   [2] p. 141.

we have two distinct methods, one electrical and the other optical, for detecting a single α-particle, and that the employment of either method may be expected to give correct results in counting the number of α-particles."[1]

Entire logical consistency cannot, perhaps, be expected in such a situation, but it remains to be recorded that, from that date onwards, for the next twenty years, Rutherford and his colleagues abandoned the electrical for the much simpler scintillation method, except in very special circumstances. Rutherford and Geiger completed their research on the number of α-particles from radium by the electrical method, but the long series of brilliant researches on the scattering of α-particles, to which we are also committed to refer at some length, was carried out entirely by the observation of scintillations.

There is a point of interest connected with the experiment on the number of α-particles which should be referred to at this stage. Ever since 1902 Rutherford had steadily held the belief that great significance was to be attached to the fact that the inert gas helium was only found, upon the earth, occluded in minerals having uranium or thorium as an important constituent. The isolation of helium was at that time a recent event and data as to its modes of association and occurrence were not widely known. Yet Rutherford had neither failed to collect these data, nor had he missed their significance. In November, 1902, in a publication [2] with Soddy, he wrote:

" In the light of these results, and the view that has already been put forward of the nature of radioactivity,

[1] p. 158.   [2] *Phil. Mag.*, November, 1902.

the speculation naturally arises whether the presence of helium in minerals and its invariable association with uranium and thorium may not be connected with their radioactivity."

At first Rutherford merely expressed the conviction that helium was an " ultimate product " of radioactive change, but his experiments on the nature of the α-radiation (p. 98) soon led him closer to the position of identifying, in his own mind at least, the actual emission of α-particles by radioactive matter with the production of helium. Though without rigorous proof, he became gradually convinced, in his own mind, that the α-particle *was* an atom of helium—carrying a charge of positive electricity and projected with very great speed. The experiment on the rate of emission of α-particles from radium, to which he had devoted so much of his time and energy, was one which, taken together with others giving the rate of production of heat, the rate of transfer of electric charge by the particles, and the electric and magnetic deflection of their paths, was drawing the net of proof closer on this most important issue. For all practical purposes, its successful conclusion provided the last piece of evidence that was required. A total of nearly five years had been spent on the general problem of the nature of the α-particle, and most people would have been fully satisfied with the final result, had it been their achievement. But, at this stage, Rutherford saw the possibility of a direct proof, and he devoted all his energies to attain it. The masterly experiment of Rutherford and Royds was the instant result.[1]   In this experiment α-particles were allowed to escape through the walls of a thin glass tube

[1] *Phil. Mag.*, February, 1909.

containing radium emanation into an outer evacuated space. From time to time the residual gases in the outer space were compressed into a minute spectrum tube and tested. After two days, the chief line in the spectrum of ordinary helium was observed; gradually the whole spectrum was obtained. Nothing could have been simpler in principle, or more convincing in the result. Every test showed that α-particles alone were needed for the production of the helium which accumulated in the outer tube: there could be no other conclusion than that when the positive charge on the particles had finally been neutralized, when they had lost their great energy of motion in producing ionization, the eventful phase of their history was ended and they lapsed for ever into the standard mode of existence of the atoms of a common gas. Indeed, nothing could have been simpler in principle, but, for this achievement, one person at least, besides Rutherford and Royds, deserves a measure of praise. In the published account of the work there is a totally unsensational passage which reads:

> " This . . . fine tube was sufficiently thin to allow the α-particles . . . to escape, but sufficiently strong to withstand atmospheric pressure. After some trials, Mr. Baumbach succeeded in blowing such fine tubes very uniform in thickness."

The success of Mr. Baumbach, the glassblower, should be remembered in connexion with this experiment of Rutherford and Royds.

From qualitative proof, Rutherford naturally passed to quantitative determination (the question " How many?" should never fall on deaf ears where a scientist is concerned). His friend Boltwood, of Yale, was spending the year in Manchester, and together they set out to measure the amount of helium produced by radium and its products in a specified time. When this had been done [1] an interesting situation arose. It was then known how many α-particles were emitted per second (about 34 million, per milligram of radium) and how much helium was produced per year (about 39 cubic millimetres per gramme, at standard temperature and pressure). Consequently nothing more than a simple calculation was needed to deduce the number of α-particles, that is helium atoms, in unit volume of gas —a standard constant of atomic chemistry. The result obtained ($2 \cdot 75 \times 10^{19}$ atoms per c.c.) should undoubtedly have been comforting to all parties concerned. It agreed with the rather uncertainly known values accepted by the chemist—and he should have seen that his atomism rested on a much surer basis in consequence —and the agreement provided further support for the essential correctness of Rutherford's own theories of radioactive disintegration, if that were needed. Thus, the man who destroyed one of the most cherished beliefs of the atomists, their belief in the indestructibility of the atom, repaid them in full—although, at the time, some were slow to appreciate the fact—by providing the most direct proof of the discrete, that is the atomic, structure of matter. Rutherford himself said:[2]

" There has been a tendency in some quarters to suppose that the development of physics in recent years has cast doubt on the validity of the atomic theory of matter. This view is quite erroneous. . . .

[1] *Phil. Mag.*, October, 1911.

[2] Presidential address, Section A, British Association, Winnipeg, 1909.

The chemical atom as a definite unit in the subdivision
of matter is now fixed in an impregnable position in
science. Leaving out of account considerations of
etymology . . . There is no assumption made that
the atom itself is indestructible and eternal. . . ."

He had already interpreted what he had seen in terms
of atoms which, with the passage of years, spontaneously
threw off one fragment after another of their own
substance; his researches were soon to lead him to
recognize other types of transformation, also, for which
outside agents were responsible.

During the days which Rutherford spent writing
up the account of the experiment with Royds, which
we have just described, word came from Stockholm
that he had been awarded the Nobel prize for chemistry
(for 1908), " as a reward of your researches on the
disintegration of the elements and the chemistry of
radioactive matters ". Earlier in the year he had
received the Bressa premium of the Academy of Sciences
of Turin, and he had also added to his number of
honorary degrees since he returned to England, but
that this new honour should overshadow the rest was
now only natural. It had been predicted for him by
his friends before he left Canada: " . . . within a
year or so I hope we may find the Nobel Committee
looking in your direction also," one of them had written
in 1904 [1]—it was now a reality. When the result was
made known, J. J. Thomson voiced a common opinion.[2]

" It is indeed splendid news . . ., no one ever deserved
it more and I am sure the award will meet with
universal approbation."

[1] Ernest Merritt, 12th November, 1904.
[2] 15th November, 1908.

To the secretary of the Swedish Royal Academy, Rutherford wrote in reply to the announcement:[1]

> " I shall be very pleased to attend the formal prize-giving and . . . to give a lecture on December 11 in the morning or afternoon, if such a time be suitable."

The delivery of a lecture, within six months of the award of the prize, is enjoined by the statutes of the Nobel foundation, and Rutherford saw no good reason to postpone its delivery. His subject was ready-made by his latest researches.

On 5th December he and Mrs. Rutherford left Manchester for Stockholm. Travelling by way of Cambridge, where they stayed one night, they arrived on 9th December. On the following day prizes were distributed by the King " in solemn assembly "—and the lecture duly took place the day after. The title given was " The chemical nature of the α-particles from radioactive substances ", and the lecture was illustrated by lantern - slides — and by experiments! At dinner at the house of Professor Mittag-Leffler, on 12th December, their host proposed the health of the new Laureates in physics (Gabriel Lippmann, of Paris) and chemistry. Some of his remarks show clearly the perplexity which he must have shared with the members of the Academy—the doubt whether radioactivity, and Rutherford's contribution to it, was the more accurately described under the one science or the other. Professor Mittag-Leffler said:[2]

---

[1] 17th November, 1908.

[2] Freely translated from the original French.

" It is an honour to me to have to welcome Mr.
Rutherford, young pioneer in that new science which
is neither physics nor chemistry, yet which is, at the
same time, both physics and chemistry. . . . Mr.
Rutherford . . . knows how to work with mathematics, the language of the sciences, he knows how
to plan and to carry out experiments; it is because
of this double ability that he has been able to unravel
so many hidden mysteries . . ., it is because of it
that many future discoveries are doubtless in store
for him, and we may hope to see him here a second
time as Laureate under the Nobel foundation."

As the years passed this last hope was never fulfilled—
on the other hand it may also be said that its lack of
fulfilment will certainly not appear as a fact sufficiently
important for consideration, in the ultimate reckonings
of Fame.

Rutherford returned to Manchester for Christmas,
and soon found himself buried in work again. Then he
began to think further about the scintillation method
and the first experiments which Geiger had done,
using this method, in the previous year. He thought,
too, about methods of detecting and counting α-particles
in general—with a most surprising result. In the New
Year he began to attend a course of lectures which
Horace Lamb, Manchester's distinguished professor
of mathematics, gave to each class of advanced students
on the theory of probability. Rutherford realized that,
in all counting experiments, in which conclusions are
drawn from the registration of a relatively small number
of particles—hundreds or thousands, only, or sometimes
considerably fewer than that—the validity of these conclusions is seriously limited by the statistical nature of

the observations. He realized that his own knowledge of the relevant mathematical theory was inadequate to meet the situation, and, Nobel Laureate or not, he took the most direct road to a better knowledge of that theory. He became a regular student again, and took notes of the lectures. Later, when he was himself more familiar with the general trend of the subject, he appealed to his first Schuster Reader in mathematical physics, H. Bateman, to work out the matter more fully with special reference to the type of problem which experiment provided.[1]

The first experiments that Geiger had done by the scintillation method in 1908 related to the scattering of α-particles in their passage through matter.[2] This, we have already noted, was experiment (7) on Rutherford's original list (p. 117) and we have marked it for further discussion. It was in 1906, when he was investigating the deflection of the paths of α-particles through the action of a strong magnetic field, that Rutherford first noticed the scattering of the particles. Generally the deflection experiments were done in a " good vacuum ", but a few tests were also made with an appreciable, though still small, amount of air in the apparatus. In these it was always found that the paths of some of the particles were slightly distorted, presumably because of the presence of the air. Then a similar " scattering " effect was observed when the particles were made to pass through a very thin sheet of mica, when the air was removed. A sheet no more than three thousandths of a centimetre in thickness caused quite a large fraction of the particles to be scattered through two degrees or more. From one point of view

[1] See *Phil. Mag.*, October, 1910.

[2] *Proc. Roy. Soc.*, August, 1908.

this was an altogether minute effect, but it did not appear so to Rutherford. He was acutely aware that no deflecting agency which he could command would produce a change of anything like two degrees in the direction of motion of the particles in so short a distance as three thousandths of a centimetre. This " would require over that distance an average transverse electric field of about 100 million volts per cm," he wrote,[1] and concluded, " Such a result brings out clearly the fact that the atoms of matter must be the seat of very intense electrical forces "—a most significant remark. Geiger had carried the original observations still farther, but at the beginning of 1909 Rutherford saw quite clearly that much more remained to be done. So Geiger and Marsden were set to work again on the problem—and within a few months they had made a most surprising discovery.[2] It was not a question this time of the deflection of the paths of the particles through one or two degrees, but a few of them—a very few in fact—were found to be deflected through more than 90 degrees, that is almost turned right-about in their paths, by quite small thicknesses of matter.

In 1909 the British Association held its meeting at Winnipeg, and Rutherford, as was most appropriate, had been chosen as president of section A. Referring to the work of Geiger and Marsden, at the end of his presidential address, he said:

" . . . recent experiments . . . show that . . . a small fraction of the α-particles, which impinge on a screen of metal, have their velocity reversed in direction and emerge again on the same side. . . . The conclusion is unavoidable that the atom is the seat

[1] *Phil. Mag.*, August, 1906. [2] *Proc. Roy. Soc.*, July, 1909.

of an intense electric field, for otherwise it would be impossible to change the direction of the particle in passing over such a minute distance as the diameter of a molecule."

When Rutherford got back to Manchester, Geiger had returned to the problem of small-angle scattering, on which he had previously been engaged, and Marsden was busy with an investigation of quite a different nature. Yet, in his moments of reflection, Rutherford was still troubled by the one α-particle in ten thousand which had its direction of motion reversed in passing through a thin gold foil. The foils which had been used were such that a few hundred atoms of gold would probably have been encountered in traversing a foil, and the results which were first obtained (in 1908) had been entirely consistent with the view that each atom contributed a small share to the actual deflection which was finally measured. Geiger's new experiments, also, were tending to confirm this statistical explanation of the small deflections which the majority of the particles suffered in traversing the foils. But for one feature, the whole phenomenon appeared to be not very different from what might have been expected on the vague views then current of the atom as an electrical system.[1] Only those few stray α-particles, which were turned back in their paths, presented a baffling problem. In scientific honesty, Geiger wrote,[2] when describing his new work:

" It is also of interest to refer here to experiments made by E. Marsden and myself on the diffuse reflection of the α-particles. It was found that some of the α-particles falling upon a metal plate . . . are

[1] See J. J. Thomson, *Proc. Camb. Phil. Soc.*, February, 1910.
[2] *Proc. Roy. Soc.*, April, 1910.

scattered to such an extent that they emerge again
on the side of incidence . . . a simple calculation,
assuming the ordinary probability law, shows that
the probability of an α-particle being scattered through
an angle exceeding 90° is extremely small and of a
different order from that which the reflection experiment suggests. It does not appear profitable at
present to discuss the assumption which might be
made to account for this difference."

It may well be that the exact shade of meaning which
the author intended (for Geiger, of course, was using
what to him was a foreign tongue) is not fully conveyed
by the last sentence of our quotation, but one interpretation, at least, is clear: if Rutherford was baffled, it
was certainly not a profitable use of time for anyone
else to discuss the significance of the facts! So, for
nearly a year longer, mere facts they remained; Rutherford could see no way through their perplexity. Then,
one day just before Christmas, 1910, all this was changed.
Geiger has written of the occasion, " he came into my
room, obviously in the best of tempers, and told me that
now he knew what the atom looked like and what the
strong scatterings signified." Rutherford had come to
the conclusion that there must be, somewhere in each
atom, an entity very much smaller than the atom
itself, containing most of the mass of the atom and
endowed with a charge of electricity, in the majority
of cases many times greater than the natural unit of
charge, the charge on the negative electron. On this
view the α-particle was itself the massive charged
portion of the helium atom — and very small in
comparison—and the unexplained large angle scattering took place on those very rare occasions when the

α-particle, in traversing an atom of matter in its path, passed very close indeed to the " nucleus " of the atom. If the law of force between charges of electricity, which Coulomb had established by large-scale experiments in the eighteenth century, still held good for such encounters as these, the explanation was numerically consistent with the facts. But the atom, of course, was left almost entirely " emptiness ", the space usually ascribed to it being populated, now, rather than filled by the elements of its structure. Clearly, a problem was bequeathed to the future in respect of this structure, but Rutherford had disposed for all time of the idea of the " solid " atom as an ultimate structural unit having any interest for physicists. Two later comments on this fundamental reorientation of outlook in physical science are typical of its impact on the larger world. Having in mind Samuel Johnson's oft-quoted rebuttal of Berkeley's idealism, Eddington wrote in 1928:[1]

" . . . what Rutherford has left us of the large stone is scarcely worth kicking."

—and Larmor, in more philosophic mood, replied to Rutherford himself, in the second year of war:[2]

" All the same my confidence in the dignity of my human nature makes me decline to believe that I personally am made up of elements that can reveal their totality of constitution even to your analysis."

And now, lest this rapid survey has left the impression that so fundamental a reorientation of outlook was accepted merely on Rutherford's own intuitive solution

[1] *The Nature of the Physical World*, 1928, p. 327.
[2] 22nd October, 1915.

of a stubborn, and isolated, problem, we must return for a while to the genesis, and testing, of the idea, before inquiring further into its consequences—into the great change which it wrought in physics itself, or in the attitude of civilized man to his world. For, when Rutherford broke in upon his assistant with the news that " he now knew what the atom looked like ", in spite of his evident elation, he did not bring mere news, so much as a challenge: he set him to work the same day on the first rough test of the theory. Remembering, much more clearly than most men would have done, the geometrical treatment of problems in particle dynamics which he had learnt fifteen years previously from a students' edition of Newton's *Principia*, Rutherford had soon worked out the main conclusions which his assumptions entailed. The conclusion which was most simply tested concerned the relative probability of scattering through various angles, and it was this aspect of the problem to which Geiger was first to direct his attention. If Rutherford's views were correct, then a certain very rapid variation with angle was to be expected—eight times as many particles scattered through angles between 60° and 120° as between 120° and 180°, to take a simple example. Geiger found precisely the variation which calculation predicted. This was a startling result: it was certainly enough for a beginning. On 7th March, 1911, Rutherford made the first public announcement of his ideas at the meeting of the Literary and Philosophical Society at Manchester, and at the same time Geiger presented his preliminary results in confirmation. In April a complete theoretical treatment was ready for dispatch to the editors of the *Philosophical Magazine*, and they saw to it that there was no delay in its publication.[1]

[1] *Phil. Mag.*, May, 1911.

As a preliminary test of the theory Rutherford had relied upon the close agreement between prediction and experiment which Geiger's results provided, but he had also submitted his ideas in various stages of their development to the friendly criticism of W. H. Bragg, then professor of physics in the University of Leeds.[1] For many years the properties of the α-particle had formed the chief topic of a long correspondence which these two physicists had carried on—at first across ten thousand miles of ocean from Adelaide to Montreal. Early in 1911, perhaps, this topic rose to its highest pitch of excitement. A few quotations from Bragg's replies during this period illustrate the tenor of the final exchanges:

On 21st December, 1910, simply, "The atom sounds fine."

On 5th January, 1911, constructive criticism, though in the lightest possible vein: " I hope you are getting on with your theory. . . . I think you will have to put some sub-centres into your atom to explain the X-ray effects."

On 12th February, just about the peak of interest: " I got your letter of yesterday just now: I have your letter of Thursday also. I am delighted to hear how things are coming out: and I agree with all you say."

Finally, on 11th March, a mere footnote, by post-card, " Campbell tells me that Nagaoka once tried to deduce a big positive centre in his atom in order to account for optical effects."

By the beginning of March, by the time that Rutherford chose to make a public announcement, therefore,

[1] Now Sir William Bragg, director of the Royal Institution.

nothing but admiration, acquiescence, and a reminder that the idea of a nuclear atom was not entirely new, remained a possible attitude for anyone who had followed the progress of its development. Let us deal with the last point first, to remove every chance of mistake. Absolute novelty cannot indeed be claimed for Rutherford's main idea, but on the other hand clear priority must be asserted for his fruitful use of the notion, in the ordering of existing data and the prediction of new effects. The very man who, according to the evidence of W. H. Bragg's postcard, first reminded him of Nagaoka's paper, later wrote in the same connexion:[1]

" . . . for the purposes of science, the author of an idea is he who first uses it to explain facts."

Explanatory scope and the power of correlating diverse phenomena, not mere similarity in verbal expression, is the sole test in these matters; if it were not so, then more attention might have to be paid to a statement of Millikan in 1904:[2]

" Since, however, no evidence has as yet appeared to show that positively charged electrons ever become detached from atoms, J. J. Thomson has brought forward the hypothesis that perhaps the positive charges constitute the nucleus of the atom, while the negative electrons are on the outside and are therefore more easily detachable."

Here it has only required the accident of a slight change in wording in what Thomson originally wrote to give a very modern ring to this statement by his reporter.

In April, 1913, the results of the further tests con-

[1] N. R. Campbell, *The Structure of the Atom*, 1923, p. vi.
[2] *Popular Science Monthly*, April, 1904.

templated in Rutherford's first account of his new theory were published in the *Philosophical Magazine*. Once more Geiger and Marsden had collaborated in these tests, and by a long series of careful experiments, occupying more than a year of patient research, they had confirmed, in every particular, the essential correctness of the notion of the nuclear atom. Only in one respect was their work incomplete: they had not investigated the scattering of α-particles in substances of lowest atomic weight. However, within a few months, Rutherford and Nuttall supplied this deficiency— though with somewhat rough observations—and then Rutherford judged the time to be ripe to " deal with certain points in connexion with the ' nucleus ' theory of the atom which were purposely omitted in my first communication on that subject." He and C. G. Darwin, his second Schuster Reader in mathematical physics, summarized the position in two papers which were published simultaneously.[1]   Everything appeared to fit into place together: certainly, by this time, one of the greatest revolutions in the history of thought in the physical sciences had been carried through, without notable opposition.   An atom-model of the nuclear type was the only one capable of explaining the experiments on α-particle scattering—and the Coulomb law of electrostatic attraction the only law which made sense in conjunction with such a model.   Yet, quite clearly, Rutherford did not believe that this conclusion marked the end of an achievement: it was only a beginning.   His remark, " The general theory would indicate that the nucleus of a heavy atom is an exceedingly complicated system, although its dimensions are very minute," points ahead to a long period of fruitful

[1] *Phil. Mag.*, March, 1914.

research, rather than back to that which had already been done.

A great deal, however, had been done in Manchester in the three years between the first and the second papers on the nuclear atom, and some of it must be referred to here. H. G. J. Moseley had taken up his experiments on X-rays, having already made very considerable contributions to the more usual " radioactive " researches of the laboratory; on the theoretical side, Niels Bohr had paid his first visit; there was much excitement in the subject of radiochemistry and many radiochemists had spent some time in Manchester to obtain the benefit of Rutherford's advice—and Rutherford himself had written yet another full-length book, *Radioactive Substances and their Radiations*, bringing the literature of the whole subject thoroughly up-to-date. The calculations of Bohr, and the experiments of Moseley and the radiochemists, all went to fill in the details of the picture which had been sketched in the first paper on the nuclear atom: all three achievements were recounted in the second paper with modest satisfaction.

The calculations which Niels Bohr made on the subject of the nuclear atom were the direct result of his visit to Manchester between April and July, 1912. Bohr had come to England some months previously and had gone first to Cambridge. He had just taken his doctor's degree in physics at Copenhagen and he had a complete year ahead of him for further study. He thought to avail himself to the full of this opportunity and decided to divide his time between the two institutions of greatest fame. Thus it was that he arrived in Manchester, from Cambridge, in April, 1912. At first, an experimental research was suggested to him—and was, in fact, begun —for Bohr had distinguished himself both in theory and in experiment in his university career, but the excitement of the new ideas soon began to work in his active mind and he was not long before he asked permission to abandon his experiment and devote his entire energies to problems of theory. Probably Rutherford never did a wiser thing than when he granted this request. In July, when he returned to Copenhagen, Bohr had already reached certain general notions of great importance—of radioactivity and gravitation as properties of the atomic nucleus, and chemical behaviour as describable in terms of the electronic structure of the atom: very soon afterwards these notions took more formal shape in his application of Planck's quantum ideas in an attempt to picture the precise arrangement of the outer electrons in the volume generally ascribed to the system. From the first, this bold treatment held Rutherford's interest and claimed his support. Until that time Planck's main ideas had not made great headway amongst physicists in general, chiefly because they appeared so restricted in application; yet it did· not appear to Rutherford such a bad thing to find new uses for them, so long as they provided some kind of answer to the less imaginative physicists of the older school, who insisted that a nuclear atom must be intrinsically unstable, according to accepted laws. Ordinary atoms were not intrinsically unstable, Rutherford would insist, as a realist: equally, experiment indicated that they must possess a type of nuclear structure. It was rather evidence in general support of quantum ideas, than conversely, that they could be used to make plausible the stability of such a structure. Sixteen years later, when Rutherford was referring to the situation which we have been discussing, he wrote:[1]

[1] *Naturwissenschaften*, 28th June, 1929.

" I was in consequence able to view with equanimity
and even to encourage Professor Bohr's bold application of the quantum theory propounded by Planck."

Underlying a conscious and rather frivolous egotism,
there can still be traced in this statement the original
belief that something important was bound to come of
the somewhat unorthodox ideas of this young Danish
mathematician.

In the late summer of 1913 Bohr published the
results of his speculations in three papers in the *Philosophical Magazine*,[1] and in 1914 he accepted Rutherford's invitation to succeed Darwin as Schuster Reader
in mathematical physics at Manchester. During the
brief period which had intervened, several fresh lines
of evidence had strengthened the already large claim
to attention which the new ideas possessed—probably
the most cogent support coming from the work of
Moseley in Manchester itself.

Moseley turned his attention to experiments with
X-rays as soon as the discovery was made [2] that naturally
occurring crystals behave rather like optical gratings in
respect of these rays. For this discovery at once provided an answer to all doubts as to the wave-nature of
the radiation, and a possible means of investigating the
wave-lengths involved. The general method had just been
outlined by W. L. Bragg, then a young student at
Cambridge, and was being put into practice at Leeds
by his father, Professor W. H. Bragg. At first, Moseley
and Darwin collaborated in the Manchester experiments, but soon Darwin became more interested in the
theory, and the collaboration ended—a wise move,

---

[1] *Phil. Mag.*, July, September, and November, 1913.
[2] By Laue, Friedrich, and Knipping, June, 1912.

probably, for thereby each made a most notable addition to knowledge in his own field. Moseley's contribution dealt with the wave-lengths of the characteristic X-rays. Some years previously, Barkla, then in Liverpool, and Kaye, in Cambridge, had established the existence of X-radiations " characteristic " of the various elements, and had shown how, in general, the penetrating power of these radiations increased as the atomic weight of the element which emitted them increased. Moseley turned the powerful new method of analysis on to these radiations. He found that the spectrum of characteristic X-rays was, with all elements, exceedingly simple, and in addition precisely similar, and he established an exact numerical relation showing how the wave-length changed from one element to another. Whatever the explanation might be, the simplicity of the phenomenon proclaimed the fundamental nature of the discovery. But the explanation, too, was not far to seek. Bohr had been able to give an amazingly accurate description of the ordinary optical spectrum of hydrogen by regarding the hydrogen atom as composed of a singly charged nucleus and a single electron. Moseley realized that much the same mathematics must apply to the case of any nucleus and the *innermost* electrons which surround it. The outer electrons need hardly be taken into account in such a calculation. If, therefore, the characteristic X-radiation were connected with the innermost electrons, only the charge on the nucleus would be responsible for the difference in wave-length from one element to another —and ultimately for the difference between the spectrum of characteristic X-radiation and its counterpart in the lightest atom, the optical spectrum of hydrogen. Moseley's empirical wave-length law then became, plausibly, a rule for giving the nuclear electric charge, from element to element. The suggestion turned out to be eminently workable. Taking the charge on the hydrogen nucleus as unit, it turned out that the charge on the nucleus of any other atom was given simply by the ordinal number which would be assigned to the atom if the chemical elements were written down in the sequence given by the periodic table of Mendeléeff. And there, too, the radiochemists came into the picture. This interpretation suited them entirely. They assented to it—and, at the same time, to the conclusion that radio-activity was a nuclear property: if an α-particle takes away two unit positive charges when expelled from a radioactive nucleus, and a β-particle one negative charge, as the interpretation requires, then the alteration in chemical properties consequent on radioactive change, and, in particular, the return to the original chemical pro-perties after the successive emission of one α-particle and two β-particles, is fully explained. Truly, every-thing appeared to fit into place together, and, in his second paper, Rutherford might well express satis-faction with the progress of his theory.

As was natural, this progress resulted in a large number of requests for lectures from all parts of the world. Rutherford had been a member of the first Solvay conference which met in Brussels late in October, 1911 (and discussed the place of quantum ideas in the theory of radiation), and two years later he was one of the eight members of the scientific committee of the conference, and its most notable figure. The topic for discussion was the structure of matter, and certainly the nuclear theory received its full share of attention in this connexion. Three years previously Rutherford had written to his mother, of a much smaller conference, also in Brussels,[1] " I took an active part and spoke on nearly all the papers ": this was more than ever true of his contribution to the Solvay conference of 1913. Then, in less than another year, an invitation from the National Academy of Sciences in Washington, and the meeting of the British Association in Australia, had taken him on brief visits not only to America but to the Antipodes, also, with the same message of triumphant achievement for his hearers. In Washington, in April, 1914, he delivered the first course of William Ellery Hale lectures on " The constitution of matter and the evolution of the elements ", and, in Melbourne, a discussion on " The constitution of the atom ", held jointly by the physics and chemistry sections, took place under his leadership on 18th August, 1914. Both these visits created great interest, but, for us, the former is the more important, for it was the occasion of the first of Rutherford's major speculations on " the evolution of the elements ". In one form or another these speculations were to occupy his attention for the rest of his life—and they were eventually to provide countless experiments for those who came to work under him. Towards the close of his lectures in Washington, Rutherford said,[2]

" Sir Norman Lockyer and others have suggested that the elements composing the star are in a state of inorganic evolution. . . . There is no doubt that it will prove a very difficult task to bring about the transmutation of matter under ordinary terrestrial conditions . . . the building up of a new atom will require the addition to the atomic nucleus of either

[1] 14th October, 1910.
[2] *Popular Science Monthly*, August, 1915.

the nucleus of hydrogen or of helium, or a combination of these nuclei. . . . It is possible that the nucleus of an atom may be altered either by direct collision of the nucleus with very swift electrons or atoms of helium such as are ejected from radioactive matter . . . under favourable conditions, these particles must pass very close to the nucleus and may either lead to a disruption of the nucleus or to a combination with it. . . . Very penetrating X-rays or gamma-rays may for similar reasons prove to be possible agencies for changing atoms."

Thus Rutherford returned from America in May, 1914, with ideas for initiating in the laboratory processes of transmutation which he was beginning to believe took place in the stars; later in the year he came home from Australia to an England at war.   Ordinarily, as 1st October drew near, he would have been drawing up his list of " researches possible "—and, almost certainly, in the list for 1914–5 attempts at transmutation would have been included in some form or another; as it was he found a laboratory rapidly emptying of those workers who had helped to make the previous years so fruitful of success.   Very soon, as the home of fundamental research at least, the place looked deserted.   For a while, the marketing, by the General Electric Company of America, of a new and much improved type of X-ray tube (the Coolidge tube) gave the necessary impetus to the continuance of a research on the production of X-rays, which Darwin had started with inferior apparatus, but even this research languished, and before long all the energies of the professor and the remaining members of his staff were absorbed in the furtherance of the national cause.

In July, 1915, there was constituted the Admiralty Board of Invention and Research, and Rutherford was invited to join the panel of the board. At that time perhaps the most pressing need of the defence forces at sea was an effective method of combating the growing menace of the submarine. The *Lusitania* had been sunk and, all vessels considered, a loss rate of about one per day had been reached. Before methods of counter-attack could be developed, reliable means of recognizing the presence of a raider, and then finding its exact position, were obviously required. Immediately, a sub-committee of the board was set up in order to investigate these problems. Rutherford was appointed to the committee and was entrusted with the task of making the preliminary report on possible methods, both of detection and location. As a result of this appointment, within a short time the laboratory at Manchester became the centre of research on under-water acoustics, and a large tank was installed on the ground-floor of the building. By November, 1915, full-scale experiments were required, and a research station was equipped at Aberdour, not far from Rosyth, where Admiralty co-operation was possible. For the next six months, Rutherford made frequent journeys to this station, and also to London for meetings of the board, and kept up a steady stream of apparatus from the laboratory at Manchester for extended tests under more nearly service conditions. Until May, 1916, he supplied most of the ideas, and the whole development depended on him for initiative. His achievement in these ten months is characteristic of his energy and genius, but it is none the less surprising, for that, that he should have been able to project himself so completely into a subject so foreign to his previous interests. In May, 1916, his responsibilities were lightened somewhat; W. H. Bragg moved to Aberdour to take charge of the work there, and Rutherford was able to concentrate more attention on the initial researches leading to future developments, and needed to devote less time to the actual supervision of the final tests on ships at sea. As the work grew in importance, as Bragg moved to the Admiralty and Eve took over a much enlarged experimental station at Harwich, Rutherford continued this work, with very valuable results. Then, in the early summer of 1917, he was asked to accompany a French scientific mission to the United States in order to put at the disposal of the new ally of the powers the results so far achieved, and to discuss with them any proposals for improvement. He was to go to Paris, first, and then forward to America with his French colleagues. " It will be an interesting trip," he wrote to his mother,[1] " but I hope to have no too exciting adventures on the way." The programme of the mission was duly carried out; works were visited, meetings were arranged with representatives of the U.S. forces, shore stations were inspected, and, after much travelling, its members reassembled in New York at the end of June for the homeward journey. By that time Rutherford had travelled even more than the rest of them, in the few weeks which they had spent in the country. He had been to Yale, and had found time to receive an honorary degree and make a speech after the ceremony, and he had also made the longer journey to Montreal to renew friendships of former times.

When Rutherford returned to Manchester in July, 1917, his main personal contribution to research on the submarine question had come to an end; practicable methods had been evolved and counter-efforts

[1] 15th May, 1917.

were beginning to bring some measure of relief, and the promise of a greater measure to come. His letters from America had shown his natural optimism less under a cloud than it had sometimes been in the months before. He still served on important committees and made frequent visits to London, in consequence, but he also began to think again of fundamental physics and snatch longer periods for experiment in the laboratory. Generally he had no one but Kay, the laboratory steward, as assistant, but the results of this work soon began to show that he was on the track of further discoveries of immense importance. He took up some experiments from the point at which Marsden had left them early in 1915.[1] Broadly speaking, the idea was to bring to the problem of α-particle scattering a new mode of attack: previously attention had been confined to the α-particles which were considerably deflected from their original paths, now the atoms which caused these deflections were to be investigated in those cases where they were given sufficient energy of motion, in the process of collision, to render them capable of individual detection by the method of scintillations. Marsden had made a beginning by observing scintillations which appeared to be due to high-speed atoms of hydrogen knocked forwards by α-particles in passing through hydrogen gas; Rutherford set himself to repeat these experiments and to extend them from hydrogen to other light elements. He had made sporadic attempts to do this from time to time during his preoccupation with the submarine problem, but on Saturday, 8th September, 1917, he took a new notebook, wrote the title "Range of high-speed atoms in air and other gases " on the flyleaf, and began a systematic investigation of the matter in hand.

[1] *Phil. Mag.*, May, 1914; August, 1915.

By Tuesday, 11th September, he had observed some unexpected scintillations when air was bombarded, and had written of them " slow absorption like H (hydrogen): cannot be C (carbon)." Obviously he had not known what to make of them, beyond this, but in the light of future developments we see that, within less than a week of beginning work in earnest, he had in fact noticed—and to some extent had already correctly interpreted — the first evidence for the artificial disintegration of a stable element in the laboratory. Yet eighteen months more were to elapse before he was sufficiently convinced of the reality of the effect, and of the validity of his interpretation, to publish the results in the ordinary way. Meanwhile, many collateral problems cropped up, and a strange, and chiefly subjective, phenomenon, simulating the appearance of " double " scintillations, diverted attention for long periods of time together. But, in the background, the new discovery was being slowly worked out: step by step, as the result of one experiment after another, the last doubts as to its significance were gradually disappearing. Amongst all the light elements, it seemed, nitrogen was definitely peculiar in this effect; no other conclusion could be accepted but that the nuclei of its atoms were indeed undergoing transmutation as a result of a very small fraction of " direct hits " scored on them by the α-particles fired through the gas. In view of the enormous importance of this conclusion—Rutherford's third great contribution to modern physics in a space of twenty years—it is interesting to follow its history farther.

On 11th September, 1917, in a matter of seven minutes counting, a total of fifty-six rather faint scintillations had been observed under conditions in which only about half as many had been expected. This was the first indication, as we have already said, that something peculiar was happening. Now, seven minutes counting would not appear a very good yield from a morning's work, if two important considerations were not allowed. First, the counting of scintillations is a most fatiguing occupation, the eye very quickly losing its sensitivity to these very faint flashes of light, unless it is frequently rested; and, secondly, the radioactive material which it was necessary to use as source of α-particles in this particular experiment was of short life, so that no more than about two hours work was possible, in any case, once a source was prepared. On Tuesday, 11th September, therefore, Rutherford had been making a preliminary survey of the effects to be observed when α-particles were fired through air under such limitations. He succeeded in counting scintillations for twenty-three one-minute periods with different metal foils in the path of the particles, and, during seven of these periods, when the greatest thickness of matter had to be traversed by the particles reaching the screen, he had expected the count to be very few indeed. Actually, during these seven periods, the numbers had been small as we have seen, but they were considerably larger than had been expected. Wondering whether this effect was peculiar to air, and if so, to what constituent of the air, on the following days Rutherford carried out similar experiments with oxygen and helium. On 28th September, after the morning's observations, he concluded briefly as follows: " Number with N (nitrogen) at same distance *twice* as great as with O (oxygen) and results agree with those on p. 9." In the afternoon, and during the following morning, carbon dioxide was used and a similar result was reached: the effect in air—due presumably to the nitrogen which it contained — was twice as great, at least, as that in helium, oxygen or carbon dioxide. After this result had been fully established, the month of October was spent chiefly in a thorough examination of the scintillations observed with the gas chamber completely exhausted and the absorbing foils used in the normal way. Then, on 7th November, the question of the " long-range scintillations from air " was taken up again and their possible origin in moisture and dust tested. But vigorous drying and filtration of the air produced no diminution in the number of scintillations. On 8th November, the number observed with clean dry air for a given strength of α-particle source was carefully determined, and on 9th November, chemically prepared nitrogen was substituted for air. An increase of about twenty-five per cent in the number of " long-range scintillations " was recorded. Obviously, now, the effect had been traced to the action of the α-particles on atoms of nitrogen: at the end of the day's work, therefore, the programme of future investigation could be outlined more clearly. In the notebook the written statement reads simply " To settle whether these scintillations are N, He, H or Li?" (See plate). High-speed nitrogen, helium, hydrogen or lithium atoms, apparently, were thought of as possible agents capable of producing scintillations under the experimental conditions—and two of these suggestions carried with them the assumption of artificial disintegration. If the scintillations were due to hydrogen atoms (as it had already been declared that their faint appearance suggested), or if atoms of lithium were concerned, these particles must have been liberated during collisions of α-particles with the ordinary atoms of nitrogen which lay in their path. Moreover, these two alternatives presumably referred, in the first case to the breaking off of the smallest possible constituent particle in the complex nitrogen nucleus, and in the second case to the splitting of the nucleus into two more or less equal fragments. It was for experiment to decide between the possibilities—but, for some months, decision proved beyond the power of experiment to achieve. On 10th January, 1918, another possibility was envisaged, and the problem receded rather than advanced on the path to solution. On that day Rutherford entered the following note in his book: " Suppose long-range scintillations in N_2 are due to atom charge $+ e$ and mass $M = 2$ called x." Suppose they are due to the liberation of an unknown kind of hydrogen atom, of double the normal mass, he was saying—that was certainly another possibility.

In spite of the difficulty of the experiment, it seemed quite clear that it would be necessary to extend to the particles producing the " long-range scintillations " the same methods of electric and magnetic deflection as had already been used to decide the precise nature of the α-particles themselves (p. 98). Yet it was a brave man who could hope to make these methods succeed in the new conditions; Rutherford achieved only partial success in their application, but by a systematic approach to the problem he at least obtained sufficient indication to confirm his original suspicions. He spent many months early in 1918 experimenting with particles which he knew to be swiftly moving hydrogen atoms (produced by simple collision processes when α-particles passed through hydrogen-rich material) and eventually he was able to show, to his own satisfaction, that the behaviour of the long-range particles from nitrogen was closely the same as that of the particles known to be hydrogen. In the following year he wrote up a connected account of all the work which he had done at odd times during the latter years of the war as four papers in the *Philosophical Magazine*,[1] and in the fourth of these papers ("An anomalous effect in nitrogen") he stated,

> "It is difficult to avoid the conclusion that the long-range atoms arising from collision of α-particles with nitrogen are not nitrogen atoms but probably atoms of hydrogen, or atoms of mass 2. If this be the case we must conclude that the nitrogen atom is disintegrated under the intense forces developed in a close collision with a swift α-particle, and that the hydrogen atom which is liberated formed a constituent part of the nitrogen nucleus."

Rutherford had subjected this idea of artificially produced nuclear disintegration to the test and criticism of direct experiment for a considerable period, and when finally it was put forward for general consideration, although the evidence was not in all points entirely conclusive, he had no longer any real doubt in the matter. Again, time has proved the soundness of his judgment: the present—already overburdened—science of nuclear physics had its origin in that short paper of six pages in the *Philosophical Magazine* of June, 1919. So another period in Rutherford's scientific career came fittingly to an end.

[1] *Phil. Mag.*, June, 1919.

Cambridge, the Second Period, 1919-1937

O N 2nd April, 1919, Sir Ernest Rutherford was elected Cavendish professor of experimental physics in the University of Cambridge. Sir Ernest Rutherford —for he had been listed Knight Bachelor amongst the New Year's Honours in 1914 — now accepted that unique scientific preferment which, by common consent, placed him in the first chair of physics in the Empire. Since our narrative was too full at the time to tell of the earlier honour, it is interesting to compare, at this stage, Rutherford's own reactions, and the reactions of his friends, to these two distinctions which added new prestige to his name.

In January, 1914, he had received, among many congratulations, the following from Larmor:[1]

> " I am not going to congratulate either you or Lady Rutherford on an incident that will hardly be heard of for weeks to come in the scenes of your international regard. I am only going to wish you many happy new years after this one: and as an obiter dictum to acknowledge that the present government . . . does manage to get good advice on scientific matters —from quarters as to which I have often had my own private guess."

[1] 1st January, 1914.

And he had replied to Stefan Meyer in the same month,[1]

" . . . I feel that such forms of decoration are highly unsuitable to youthful and relatively impecunious professors! However, I expect the sympathy of all my scientific friends as a martyr in the cause of science."

April, 1919, on the other hand, brought congratulations in a different vein. John Cox wrote:[2]

" So you are there at last! . . . It was 1898, wasn't it, when I fished you out of the Cavendish, and it has taken you just 20 years to come back to be its master. I've been trying to recall all you have put into those 20 years—enough to justify the result a dozen times. You remember saying at McGill that you would not leave unless either Manchester or Cambridge came open and that neither was likely? And now you have had both."

With Rutherford, too, in 1919, the whole case was altered. It was no merely formal reply which he then addressed to the Senate of the University of Manchester thanking them for their message of farewell. Formality was done away with in favour of intimacy, as was characteristic of the man; it was also set on one side as inadequate, when deeper issues were involved. Rutherford wrote,[3]

" At the last meeting of the Senate I was in the embarrassing position of having to listen to the friendly dissection of my life and character by repre-

[1] 17th January, 1914.   [2] 7th April, 1919.
[3] 2nd June, 1919.

sentatives of the Senate, without the right to reply. Now that I have recovered from the ordeal, I would like to take the opportunity of thanking the Senate —individually and collectively—for their very kind and appreciative resolution.

" I have passed a very happy and fruitful twelve years in your midst and I am sure no one could have been treated with more kindness and consideration than has been shown by all my colleagues. I do not take any credit to myself for services to the University, for I only gave my best as I am sure do all my colleagues. I have been proud to belong to the University of Manchester and my appreciation of the sterling character of its work for the community has grown with closer acquaintance. I will, I am sure, for some time to come, find it very difficult not to regard Manchester as the most progressive of our universities. While I am leaving many close friends behind me, I hope that my departure from Manchester will not lead to a complete severance of my ties with this university. I shall watch its future development with interest and sympathy and if I can be of any help in promoting its welfare, I should be only too glad to assist in any way I can. All universities, whether young or old, face similar problems to-day and in order to reach our greatest usefulness we must learn to help one another and work together more in the future than in the past. We are all members of the same brotherhood and as far as I am concerned I shall try to work for an ' entente cordiale ' between the two universities with which I am connected.

" It is with feelings of very great regret that I shall part from my colleagues. I shall miss the pleasant converse of the smoking room and the oratory of ancient days of the Senate. I shall, on the other hand, carry with me from Manchester pleasing recollections of many a lively skirmish and of many a well-contested fight that I have been privileged to witness in the council chamber."

So Ernest Rutherford passed forward to Cambridge, to his attack on the nucleus.

On his previous appointments, at Montreal and at Manchester, Rutherford had been greatly fortunate, as we have seen, in that he was able to take up his own researches from the point which they had reached, with the minimum of delay. On his return to Cambridge, once again he made sure that similar opportunities offered, but on this occasion, more than ever before, he found, also, problems of departmental reorganization to claim a share of his attention. He met both problems, the scientific and the administrative, with equal energy and thoroughness. He returned to Cambridge not without a certain suspicion of the friendliness of the old order towards the advance of his science, but he was not thereby deterred from the bold statement of his requirements for its efficient prosecution. He came to a businesslike agreement with the retiring professor (Thomson had been appointed to succeed H. M. Butler as Master of Trinity, and so had resigned the professorship), and he drew up a memorandum on the needs of the department for presentation to the university. For its greater effectiveness, he prefaced this memorandum by a detailed *History of the Cavendish Laboratory*, written separately with compelling force. The conclusions of the memorandum are as surprising as, on closer examination, they appear logical and necessary. They are surprising because the recommendations do not touch Rutherford's own researches in the slightest degree; they are logical, at least, because it is clearly evident that, within the laboratory as he found it, Rutherford was confident that there was space enough for his own researches to be effectively carried out. But there were other desirable activities, apparently, for which he regarded the provision as entirely inadequate.

The memorandum concluded:

" The most pressing and urgent needs for the department to make it thoroughly efficient are summarized below:

(1) Increased laboratory and lecture space for the teaching of Physics.

(2) Provision of new, well-equipped laboratories for Applied Physics, Optics and Properties of Matter.

(3) Provision of three additional lecturers of high standing, competent to direct advanced study in research in the new departments mentioned above.

(4) The endowment of another Chair of Physics in the University.

. . . . It is estimated that the cost of the new buildings would be not more than £75,000 and that an additional sum of £125,000 will be necessary as an adequate endowment . . ."

Needs (2) and (3) are set out in greater detail earlier in the memorandum, where the trend of the argument may be gauged from the following quotation: " The need of a laboratory specially devoted to training in research in Applied Physics is of pressing importance if we are to play our part in the researches required by the State, and in providing well-qualified research men for various branches of industry and for the scientific departments of the State." But the university was not entirely convinced, and the money was not available: as events proved, Rutherford had to wait until the last years of his life before plans for the extension of the laboratory and its activities, in which sums of the order of a quarter of a million pounds were involved, could be seriously considered.

In comparison with the results of his efforts towards departmental reorganization, Rutherford's attack on the problem of the nucleus of the atom had more immediate success. He brought with him a considerable amount of apparatus from Manchester in a form ready for use, he brought the large quantity of radium lent him by the Academy of Sciences of Vienna in 1908, he brought with him one of his research students, James Chadwick, who was accepted as Wollaston Student at Gonville and Caius College—and he would have brought with him Kay, his laboratory steward, also, had he not given way chiefly on a domestic issue which he considered important (". . . his wife was averse to leaving her friends, so I advised him to stay where he was," Rutherford later wrote to Boltwood[1]). Finally, Rutherford brought to Cambridge, what he was never for long without, a list of twenty or thirty " projected researches "—scribbled in pencil[2] on the back pages of an old laboratory notebook. Within a

[1] 2nd November, 1920.   [2] 18th February, 1919.

few months of his appointment, therefore, he was able to write to Stefan Meyer,[1]

> " I brought down your radium with me and have been able to start my investigations again on the nitrogen problems. . . . I am hopeful that I will be able to settle the question definitely before long. . . . If the atom is not disintegrated by α-particles I am of the opinion it will not be done in our time."

Soon, the hoped-for results began to accrue, but certain difficulties also became increasingly apparent.   In August he wrote to Boltwood,[2]

> " I wish I had a live chemist tied up to this work who could guarantee on his life that substances were free from hydrogen. With this little detail set on one side, I believe that I could prove very quickly which of the lighter elements give out hydrogen, but it is very difficult to do so without the chemical certainty as the effect is so small."

— When these researches had progressed only so far that Rutherford had confirmed his original findings with nitrogen, he was invited to give his second Bakerian lecture before the Royal Society.   This lecture was published in the Proceedings of the Society in July, 1920. It has become famous for the uncanny accuracy of the speculations which it contains regarding the fundamental units and patterns of structure of the nuclei of atoms. Not only the neutron, but the hydrogen isotope of mass 2 (the deuteron) also, are to be found in its pages, twelve years before they were detected in a

[1] 13th January, 1920.   [2] 19th August, 1920.

laboratory experiment (see p. 178). The central statement of this oft-quoted example of high scientific prophesy took the following form:

> " If we are correct in this assumption it seems very likely that one electron can also bind two H nuclei and possibly also one H nucleus. In the one case, this entails the possible existence of an atom of mass nearly 2 carrying one charge, which is to be regarded as an isotope of hydrogen. In the other case, it involves the idea of the possible existence of an atom of mass 1 which has zero nucleus charge. . . ."

Many a would-be prophet might have stopped here, half-afraid of the creature of his own imagination, but Rutherford had no such fear. He continued:

> " Such an atom would have very novel properties. Its external field would be practically zero, except very close to the nucleus, and in consequence it should be able to move freely through matter . . . it should enter readily into the structure of atoms, and may either unite with the nucleus or be disintegrated by its intense field. . . . The existence of such atoms seems almost necessary to explain the building up of the nuclei of heavy elements; for unless we suppose the production of charged particles of very high velocities it is difficult to see how any positively charged particle can reach the nucleus of a heavy atom against its intense repulsive field."

During the year 1920 two separate investigations were set on foot in the Cavendish Laboratory in order to look for evidence of this hypothetical atom—the neutron

—but they gave negative results. Yet Rutherford never wholly abandoned the idea, and we shall see how, when the first real hint of the existence of the neutron appeared in the results of experiments (p. 178), his colleagues already shared his foresight sufficiently to be well-trained to appreciate its significance.

Even before the Bakerian lecture was published, other physicists besides Rutherford had been speculating along somewhat similar lines regarding the structure of nuclei —and it is of interest to review briefly the relation between some of their work and that of Rutherford himself. In Melbourne, cut off, as a colonial professor often is, from the more stirring ideas inspiring contemporary research, Orme Masson had devised a " model " for the nucleus, with neutrons and deuterons—and other particles—as units of structure. He wrote up his ideas and submitted them to Rutherford for his criticism. Friendly letters followed, and eventually a paper was published in the *Philosophical Magazine* [1] with an explanatory footnote which Rutherford contributed. In his letter of thanks Masson wrote,[2] " I have not yet seen Harkins's paper in the *Phys. Review*, to which you refer." Harkins, of Chicago, was the other chief claimant to the independent suggestion of the ideas with which we are concerned—and the paper of his which Rutherford had mentioned was one which had appeared in America as early as February, 1920. The same paper was also in question when Harkins himself wrote to Rutherford on 6th December, 1920. In the course of a long letter he said,

" I was very much interested to note that you consider the possibility of the existence of an element of

[1] February, 1921.   [2] 7th January, 1921.

zero atomic number, especially since I made this suggestion in a paper sent to the *Physical Review* more than a year ago. It would certainly be of great interest if you could detect such particles, which could hardly be very abundant on the earth's surface."

Here we see quite clearly that similar notions concerning the structure of nuclei were, in fact, beginning to be entertained in various parts of the world, and that, in one sense, their origins were independent. In view of this conclusion, it is characteristic of Rutherford's fairness in such matters that he never wished to deny this independence—witness his sponsoring of Masson's paper —but it is also characteristic of his individual estimate of the strength of his own position that he should write, some months later, to Boltwood,[1] on this very subject,

"Actually, however, most of the ideas . . . have been common property in this country and especially to myself for the last five years. It is exceedingly easy to write about these matters, but exceedingly difficult to get experimental evidence to form a correct decision."

"Especially to myself" is the true Rutherford touch— but it is not an overstatement, for we have already seen (p. 144) that he had been active in speculation on the problem since he prepared his Hale lectures for delivery at Washington in April, 1914.

Of the Bakerian lecture, Jacques Loeb wrote,[2]

"The most wonderful part is that it looks as if you were just entering on a new series of scientific

[1] 28th February, 1921.   [2] 31st August, 1920.

conquests. Well, it is good to have lived and read these things even in the midst of all the misery which politicians, generals and capitalists have settled on the world."

—and, later in the same letter, after a reference to the growing hold of bureaucracy on scientific research in his own country,

" I am under the impression that your Bakerian lecture will do more for science than all the National Research Councils in the world put together."

Such eulogy as this was not lavished on any other of the somewhat similar speculations published at that time.

Less than three years later, Loeb wrote again to Rutherford,[1]

" It is perfectly amazing how rapidly you are settling the problems of atomic and nuclear structure. I still remember one afternoon in Berkeley [2] I heard you give a forecast of the planetary atom such as you have shown it to-day to be a reality; but that in these few years you should also have succeeded in solving the problem not only of the electronic structure but also of the nuclear structure takes one's breath away. I do not think any man in the history of science has been able to make the progress that you have made in a comparatively short number of years."

This is fulsome praise indeed—to be judged less hardly, perhaps, because Loeb was not a physicist—but it is not mere flattery. The disintegration experiments were be-

---

[1] 10th May, 1923.
[2] This must have been in July, 1906 (cf. p. 109).

ginning to give reproducible results, and six of the lighter elements, at least, had been shown capable of disintegration. A " live chemist " had not been " tied up to the work ", but a method of avoiding the necessity of his services was in course of development [1]—an entirely preferable solution. Then C. D. Ellis had been given the task of taking up the pre-war investigations of Rutherford, Robinson and Rawlinson on the β and γ radiations, which until then had been relatively neglected —and important results were emerging. In no sense could the problem of nuclear structure be regarded as solved—as Loeb had implied—but, at least, the real attack had at last begun. By the time that Rutherford had to deliver his Liverpool address, as President of the British Association in September, 1923, he had begun to repent the lack of faith which had marked some of his earlier opinions. He confessed,

" In a discussion on the structure of the atom ten years ago, in answer to a question on the structure of the nucleus, I was rash enough to say that it was a problem that might well be left to the next generation, for at that time there seemed to be few obvious methods of attack to throw light on its constitution."

When he had once seen the possibility of such an attack, however, Rutherford certainly was not content to leave the problem entirely to the next generation.

Yet the younger generation played a very important part indeed in Rutherford's successful advance beyond the bounds which he had earlier thought to be impassable. At Montreal, a handful of earnest young researchers had acknowledged as their obvious leader one of their own

[1] See Rutherford and Chadwick, *Proc. Phys. Soc.*, August, 1924.

age and interests; in the latter days at Manchester, and at Cambridge, that leader had advanced in years and grown in renown; he had become " Papa " to his youthful colleagues, but he still retained as much of their affection, and shared in their adventures almost as closely, as in former times. Both sides of the picture appear clearly in the following quotations. Answering an invitation to deliver a course of lectures in the United States in 1923, Rutherford wrote to Boltwood,[1]

" It is a pity but I cannot go. I am bound to the wheel with my laboratory. . . . I should very much like to be free to spend a few weeks in Yale again . . . but life for me is very busy in these days and I have to drive the boys along."

Then Ellis wrote of the inspiration of his professor's companionship, during the long periods of inactivity which had necessarily to be observed in the disintegration experiments, when scintillations were being counted,[2]

" Sitting there, drinking tea, in the dim light of a minute gas jet at the farther end of the laboratory, we listened to Rutherford talking of all things under the sun."

His " boys " were the agents through whom Rutherford attained many of his later triumphs; that they were his willing agents no further proof is required.

When we speak of the triumphs of Rutherford and his school in fundamental research, the period 1925–30 is apt to appear unproductive and uninteresting. There is a sense in which this is a true estimate of his achieve-

---

[1] 30th May, 1922. [2] Obituary notice, *Proc. Phys. Soc.*, May, 1938.

ment in those years, but there is a deeper sense in which it does much less than justice to that achievement. Two considerations are all-important in this connexion.

In the first place, ever since the disintegration experiments of 1919 had emphasized the pressing need for a theory of nuclear structure—over and above the mere recognition of the existence of the nucleus of the atom —experimenters had worked completely unaided by the suggestions which such a theory should normally provide; for there was, in fact, no mathematical theory of the building of nuclei. In a new subject, perhaps, the lack of a guiding theory is a disadvantage which may be disregarded for a time, but, eventually, experiment loses direction unless some degree of theoretical synthesis is achieved. In the subjects of radioactivity and nuclear physics the first emergence of such a synthesis is not to be found until the years 1928 and 1929.

Then, in the second place, and more importantly from our viewpoint, the period 1925–30 was one of comparative unproductiveness just because the methods of experiment currently adopted were beginning to reach the limits of their usefulness. We have already stressed the slowness and the subjective limitations of the method of counting scintillations: a controversy with the workers in Vienna at the beginning of our period (1925–6), concerning the results of disintegration experiments obtained in this way, quickened Rutherford's desire to see developed a much more objective and more rapid method of attack. Through his encouragement, by the end of this period, C. E. Wynn Williams[1] had succeeded in working out a trustworthy electrical (radiovalve) method of recording, which was well advanced towards perfection. Again, in a slightly different line of

[1] Following Greinacher, in Switzerland.

advance, and in the end more spectacularly, attempts were well under way to produce streams of particles artificially accelerated to high speeds, in order to replace the α-particles from radioactive sources as projectiles for atom bombardment. In this line of work T. E. Allibone and E. T. S. Walton were pioneer experimenters, under Rutherford's inspiration. After he had spent the whole of his scientific life as the exponent of the most simple and direct methods of experimentation, Rutherford was thus, in the end, compelled by circumstances to apply himself to what he generally called "engineering physics". Nevertheless, it must be remarked how thorough, and finally how successful, that application of his interests was, once the decision had been made—and, again, in fairness to his prevision, how clearly he foresaw the necessity of keeping such large-scale developments in view. In September, 1919, he inquired of the research department of the General Electric Company of America concerning the construction of a transformer for 2000 cycles and 100,000 volts, and thereafter he was kept in close contact with the many important advances in technical physics which originated in their laboratory. It was in the course of this correspondence that Dr. A. W. Hull wrote to him,[1]

"We are very much excited about your experiments on aluminium, &c., and about Dr. Langmuir's report of Ellis's work. Dr. Coolidge wants to make a 3,000,000 volt X-ray tube in order to manufacture radium C gamma rays. Up to date he has gone as far as 300,000 volts and expects soon to be operating at 400,000 volts."

[1] 3rd December, 1921.

Before long, other electrical firms, nearer home, were interested, also, and Rutherford lost no opportunity of encouraging their interest.

On 30th November, 1927, Dr. W. D. Coolidge received the Hughes Medal of the Royal Society and Rutherford was in the chair. We can gauge the difficulty of the aim which, six years previously, Coolidge had proposed to himself, and something of his perseverance in pursuing it, from some of the remarks which Rutherford made on that occasion. He said,

> "Taking advantage of the great improvements in vacuum technique and the ease of supply of electrons from a glowing filament, Dr. Coolidge has constructed an electron tube which will stand 300,000 volts. . . . It has not so far been practicable to apply much more than 300,000 volts to a single tube . . . experiments have been made with three tubes in series and 900,000 volts, giving a supply of electrons corresponding to one or two milliamperes through the thin window in the last tube."

Insight into Rutherford's own interest in the development of the subject can also be obtained from the same address. Thus,

> "It has long been my ambition to have available for study a copious supply of atoms and electrons which have an individual energy far transcending that of the α- and β-particles from radioactive bodies. I am hopeful that I may yet have my wish fulfilled, but it is obvious that many experimental difficulties will have to be surmounted before this can be realized, even on a laboratory scale."

and again,

" While no doubt the development of such high voltages serves a useful technical purpose, from the purely scientific point of view interest is mainly centered on the application of these high potentials to vacuum tubes in order to obtain a copious supply of high-speed electrons and high-speed atoms. . . . This would open up an extraordinarily interesting field of investigation which could not fail to give us information of great value, not only on the constitution and stability of atomic nuclei but in many other directions."

So the researches of Allibone, Walton and others, which he fostered in Cambridge, are to be explained. These researches provided no immediate data of fundamental importance, but within a few years they were to develop very much in the way that Rutherford had foreseen for them.

During the period which we have been describing, Rutherford was also fostering in Cambridge researches on an engineering scale which had nothing at all to do with his own investigations concerning the nuclei of atoms. In 1921 Peter Kapitza came to England, having been for three years lecturer in physics at the Polytechnical Institute in Petrograd. Originally, Kapitza had been trained as an electrical engineer, and, after a year with Rutherford carrying out an experiment on α-particles involving the measurement of minute quantities of heat, he was given every chance to apply his earlier training. He began a series of investigations concerning the possibility of obtaining, for short periods of time, magnetic fields several times stronger than those reached in the normal operation of the most powerful electromagnets. Grants were obtained for these researches, and a special laboratory was fitted up in an old building vacated by the department of chemistry. Preliminary experiments were successful, and Rutherford was deeply impressed by the importance of the work. Further grants were negotiated for the construction of more robust apparatus, and many important results emerged. Kapitza was elected to a fellowship at Trinity College, and a small band of research students was got together to work under his personal direction. He became F.R.S., and in 1930 was offered and accepted a Messel research professorship administered by the Royal Society. At the same time an arrangement was made for the building of a permanent laboratory for magnetic and low-temperature research, attached to the Cavendish Laboratory, in which his work should be done. The Royal Society once more provided the initial capital (from the income of a bequest left them in 1923 by Dr. Ludwig Mond), and the university agreed to be responsible for maintenance. Nothing could be more obvious than that, throughout all these developments, Rutherford had been the efficient champion of work in which he had a genuine, though not a directly personal, interest. In an intimate moment he once said, "The Royal Society has grown to be a fabulously wealthy institution—and I have the greatest difficulty in preventing almost the whole of the proceeds from gravitating in Cambridge!" Another, and more sober, version of his influence on the finances of the society is given in his farewell address as president, on 1st December, 1930. He said,

"It would, therefore, seem that the time has arrived when we may with prudence consider how some at any rate of the accumulated income of our trust funds may best be expended in promoting some form of scientific research. . . . In considering the best method of utilizing the balance of the Society's present resources, the Council . . . after careful consideration, were impressed by the fundamental importance of the researches at present being carried on by Dr. P. Kapitza, at Cambridge, and the need for continuing this work on a more permanent basis. . . . After full consideration, therefore, the Council, in addition to appointing Dr. Kapitza to a Messel Professorship, agreed to offer the University of Cambridge a sum of £15,000, for the building of a suitable laboratory. . . ."

In the face of such statesmanship, nothing that Rutherford could do, besides, could prevent the wealth of scientific talent from gravitating within the circle of his influence!

Just before he was called to the Presidency of the Royal Society, in 1925, Rutherford had been created a member of the Order of Merit; soon after he relinquished that office towards the end of 1930, his name was to be found included amongst those of the new peers in the January Honours List. One may sense the naturalness—almost the inevitableness—of it all, in the eyes of his friends, from a letter of Horace Lamb on the former occasion,[1]

" I am delighted to see that you are at last enrolled among the greater gods. . . . There is nothing left but a peerage!"

On that occasion, A. E. Housman, too, had added his testimony. As a fellow-member of the High Table at

[1] 1st January, 1925.

Trinity College, as Rutherford knew him, he voiced his congratulations in a different vein.   With one eye on the Antipodes—and his tongue in his cheek—he wrote,[1]

" This is a sad day for poor old England, and will put new and unnecessary pep into the All Blacks; but I am afraid there was no avoiding it . . . if a Trinity prime minister had failed to do his duty he would have been unpopular in Trinity.   Long may you live to enjoy your honour."

Elevation to the peerage brought with it the problems of title and arms, and to these Rutherford gave his usual deep consideration, taking advice on each point from those friends who were best able to help him. Finally, he decided to hold his Barony " of Nelson, New Zealand "; then, after some little delay, letters patent were granted for the coat-of-arms which he and his friends had devised.   It is not our purpose here to enter into the full heraldic details of these arms, but we might mention, in passing, that they included a representation of the kiwi, as crest, indicating Rutherford's connexion with New Zealand, and that the shield was divided simply by crossed curves recalling his early formulation of the disintegration theory.   The original rise and decay curves of the thorium X activity (see p. 84) provided the idea for this quartering.

Rutherford made his maiden speech in the House of Lords on 20th May, 1931.   A question had been put down on the Order Paper for that day, " Whether the Government can give information on the scientific investigations by the Department of Scientific and Industrial Research on the production of oil from coal,"

---

[1] 1st January, 1925.

and Rutherford, as the recently appointed chair-man of the advisory council of that department, was the natural authority to whom the Government turned for a reply. The speech was a great success—" Your speech was splendid and your voice much more clear and resonant than that of any other speaker," Elliot Smith wrote afterwards.[1] There was an ease and a generality—and a complete absence of any sense of condescension—in Rutherford's treatment of scientific problems for the benefit of the layman, on all occasions, and this maiden speech provides a good example of the best of his popularizations. We may indicate its tenor by brief quotation:

> " While I cannot claim to have any expert knowledge in this difficult field of research I have endeavoured to acquaint myself with the details of the work now in progress. . . . I should like to put before you some considerations of a general character with which you will be familiar. . . . Before dealing with the processes concerned I would like to mention some general economic considerations . . my interest in this problem is mainly on the scientific side. . . . It is not my province to speak on the policy that should be adopted to encourage or assist the commercial production of oil from coal, but I should like to point out that a sound policy can only be formulated in the light of knowledge. . . . While [economic and political circumstances] may, and will, change from time to time, and so properly lead to changes in policy, the scientific facts remain unaltered. . . . Research is in essence the exploration of the unknown, and it is impossible to forecast the results of experiment.

[1] 21st May, 1931.

Research is likely to be more fruitful when guided by views or theories based on previous knowledge. Whether such views prove correct or not, the work cannot fail to add to knowledge, and in many cases may produce results of value in quite unexpected directions. Even negative results may in some cases prove as valuable as positive ones, for they may prevent the waste of money in attempts to develop processes which are fundamentally unsound."

It is abundantly clear that the members of the House of Lords heard more than the mere answer to a particular question late in the afternoon of 20th May, 1931 —and it is clear, also, why one of his friends should write to him, on another and later occasion,[1]

" Whatever the real topic I hope you will be able to take part and speak authoritatively for Science."

During the last ten years of his life, Rutherford's claim to be heard with deference, on any of the broad issues in which science is involved, passed entirely without challenge.

In the domestic councils of scientists, during this period, Rutherford was an equally commanding figure, but here his views were more often submitted to criticism, and were occasionally opposed. He relished a contest, however, and was quite open in his admission of the fact. After a particularly heated meeting, he wrote to a friend and colleague,[2]

" I have asked H—— to tell you about the field day I had yesterday where I was like Daniel in the

[1] N. V. Sidgwick, 10th July, 1936.
[2] Sir F. E. Smith, 14th November, 1935.

Lion's Den—but all the same Daniel came out pretty well unscathed."

Again, to the same correspondent, three days earlier,[1] he had written of another encounter,

" I got thoroughly fed up with it and gave them my views without much reticence."

There were times, certainly, when Rutherford was the scientist militant, and mid-November, 1935 was evidently one of them! In the summer of 1934 the New Zealand Fruit Board had marked a definite stage in its history by asking Rutherford, as the most famous of all New Zealanders, to accept as a personal gift the millionth case of apples exported by the dominion. Arthur Smithells wrote to him then,[2]

" It is a very happy idea to make you the recipient of the millionth box of apples . . . speaking as your father-confessor, I cannot forget the amount of the old Adam which I have found in you."

But he, too, had also written, a few weeks previously,[3]

" R—— told me that you had flattered him by saying that he made a noise like a physicist. . . . I would almost say that you sometimes *sound* like a saint."

Rutherford's occasional bursts of fierce indignation were much less frequently tinged with real animosity than they were incurred by obvious incompetence or humbug.

[1] 11th November, 1935.　　[2] 7th July, 1934.
[3] 18th May, 1934.

We have spoken, already, of the period 1925–30 as one in which improvements in experimental technique rather than fundamental discoveries in nuclear physics were made by Rutherford's colleagues and students in the Cavendish Laboratory. If this is a true evaluation of achievement, then, equally, the year 1932 was rich in fulfilment and return. In that year the neutron was finally discovered with the properties which Rutherford had predicted for it (see p. 161), and, for the first time, the disintegration of the nuclei of atoms was brought about by means of fast-moving charged particles "artificially" accelerated by the application of high voltages to a vacuum tube. Both these achievements belong essentially to the Cavendish Laboratory, and it can justly be claimed that, as a result of them, 1932 marks the beginning of a new era in the science of nuclear physics. Rutherford was only to live to see the first five and a half years of this era, but the extent of the advance, which that short period witnessed, was surely enough to satisfy him that his policy in research direction in earlier years had been amply rewarded. As soon as the initial success had been achieved, he immediately threw the whole of his energy into assuring that adequate means for following up the new discoveries were available for his younger colleagues. Also, he returned, himself, after what had been the lapse of a year or two, to take a personal share in the prosecution of particular researches. Once more his brain became active in speculation and his old enthusiasms were aroused anew. During the next few years he never tired of recounting, in popular lectures at the Royal Institution and elsewhere, the startling results which his "boys" were obtaining. It was in just this way that the first full details of the discovery of the neutron, and some of the earliest results concerning disintegration by fast protons and deuterons,[1] were made available to the public.

Rutherford's announcement of the results of the neutron experiments was made at a Friday evening discourse at the Royal Institution on 18th March, 1932. The first part of this lecture had dealt with matters of topical interest, certainly, but with matters of general knowledge among physicists; the second part was reserved for the more startling disclosures. In that half-hour Rutherford told of the work of Bothe and Becker in Germany, and Curie and Joliot in Paris, and of its repetition and extension by H. C. Webster under Chadwick's direction in Cambridge. All this work had shown that a penetrating radiation of somewhat unusual properties was emitted when the metal beryllium was bombarded by the α-particles from radioactive elements. Hydrogen nuclei (protons) were not emitted —as they were from several light elements such as nitrogen and aluminium—but the general conclusion appeared to be that a type of γ-radiation was emitted, instead. Then, he said,

> " In examining the absorption of this beryllium radiation by the ionization method, Mme Curie-Joliot and M. Joliot made the striking observation that hydrogen material, when exposed to this radiation, emitted swift protons."

—and he went on to describe how this observation had provided the one clue, lacking until then, which was sufficient to convince Chadwick that neutral particles,

[1] The existence of the deuteron—the hydrogen nucleus of mass two —had been established by Urey in America in the autumn of 1931.

rather than radiations of the γ-ray type, were responsible for most of the effects. Within a few days Chadwick had confirmed his suspicion by direct numerical test of the alternative hypotheses, on the basis of new experiments of his own, and thereafter the neutron of mass one, the neutron of Rutherford's Bakerian lecture of 1920, was established as one of the fundamental entities of the physicist's world.

The experiments carried out at Cambridge in the previous month had not stopped at this conclusion. Rutherford continued,

> " Very valuable information can be obtained by photographing the effects due to the passage of this new type of radiation through a Wilson expansion chamber. A number of such experiments have been made by N. Feather and P. I. Dee in the Cavendish Laboratory in association with Dr. Chadwick. . . . Feather . . . has observed another very interesting effect . . . he has obtained photographs . . . which indicate that the nitrogen nucleus has disintegrated in a novel way. . . . It will take time to analyse the results obtained, and to examine the effects produced in other gases. The peculiar properties of the neutron allow it to approach closely, or even to enter, nuclei of high atomic number, and it will be of great interest to study the effects of such collisions. It is, however, evident that this new radiation has surprising properties, and there is every promise that it may prove an effective agent in extending our knowledge of the artificial disintegration of elements."

The experiments, we see, had progressed rapidly, but Rutherford's scientific imagination had gone forward even more rapidly still. In 1920 he had been twelve years ahead of experiment with his speculation; even in 1932, with the pace of research faster by far, in this concluding passage he was expressing ideas which were fully two years in advance of the important experiments which Fermi was to perform in 1934.

On 4th November, 1932, Rutherford delivered the nineteenth Thomas Hawksley lecture before the Institution of Mechanical Engineers. He chose for his title " Atomic projectiles and their applications ", and once again he reserved for the closing stages of the lecture the tit-bit of the evening. On this occasion it concerned the work of Cockcroft and Walton on the disintegrations produced by accelerated protons. Over a period of two years Cockcroft and Walton had collaborated in developing a method of maintaining a steady source of high potential from which a small direct current could be drawn, and in building a sectional vacuum tube which would stand the potential difference (up to 800,000 volts) which they were able to maintain. By means of this apparatus they had obtained a current of protons accelerated through this difference of potential and had bombarded a number of elements with these fast-moving projectiles. In addition to other less definite results, they had reported large numbers of disintegration particles from the light elements lithium, boron and fluorine. Rutherford had been keenly interested, himself; he had been called in to examine the scintillations produced by these particles and had seen the tracks which they produced in the expansion chamber. He guessed that they were α-particles. Cockcroft and Walton had been able to confirm his suspicions by quantitative investigations. He concluded his lecture by saying,

" It seems clear that this new method of attack, so successfully begun by Cockcroft and Walton, will in the course of the next decade give us much new information on the structure of nuclei and the problem of the transmutation of the elements. We have seen that the bombardment by α-particles leads to the building up of nuclei of heavier mass, while the bombardment by the neutron and the proton in general seems to result in disintegration which lowers the mass of the nucleus. A close comparison of the transformation effects . . . cannot fail to give us new information. . . . It is obvious also that the results to be obtained by these methods will help us to understand the processes of production and destruction of nuclei which must occur in the interior of our sun or other hot stars under the influence of the swiftly-moving nuclei of different kinds which arise from thermal agitation. . . ."

Such flights as this are not the products of an earthbound imagination!

As we have indicated, the year 1932 saw merely the beginning of a revival of interest in the subject of nuclear physics, and here we cannot follow detailed developments farther. By the end of the year, a formidable array of powerful apparatus had been assembled in many laboratories throughout the world—and much more was soon to be added; also several new particles had been recognized as products or agents in the transmutation of nuclei. In the years that followed, work went ahead at a great rate. If the reader wishes to learn more of this from Rutherford's own pen, he should turn to the published accounts of his lectures—and particularly to that of the Henry Sidgwick Memorial

Lecture at Newnham College, put out in book form as
The Newer Alchemy, a few months before Rutherford
died. In the preface to this slender volume we read,

" Since the early days of Radioactivity, the problem
of the transmutation of the elements has occupied
much of my attention, and I have followed with
the greatest interest and enthusiasm the remarkable
increase in our knowledge that has come so rapidly
in the last few years."

Since 1937, the pace of that increase has not slackened,
and we can be quite sure that Rutherford's enthusiasm
would not have lagged, either, had he been alive to-day.
His last direct contact with the laboratory which had
been the scene of his triumphs for so many years took
place about 6 o'clock in the evening of Thursday, 14th
October, 1937, when the present writer obeyed his
instructions to find out and to telephone him the day's
results in a rather trivial experiment, which for a time
had seemed to possess considerable interest. There was
nothing of importance to report, but his last words
were words of interest and encouragement, all the same.
Five days later he died, at the height of his renown.
He had been at the laboratory a week previously, then
a busy day in London; the first forebodings of illness
that Wednesday night; Thursday at home, dealing
with laboratory correspondence in the morning, discussing lectures with me—now his biographer—over
tea; on Friday the trouble diagnosed, the nursing
home, in the evening an operation, with every care—
.and then, on Tuesday, 19th October, a peaceful end.
Suddenly the laboratory was without its leader—and
it began to realize its loss.

Six days later, with quiet dignity, in the sight of a

great congregation of eminent and humble men, the last remains of Ernest, 1st Baron Rutherford of Nelson, were laid, near the graves of Newton and Kelvin, in Westminster Abbey. Honour was thereby done to his memory, but, if greater honour could have been done, his fellow-countrymen would not have denied him it.

Chapter 7

Epilogue

IT has often been said that it is a happy end for a man to die at the height of his powers; not to know the slow decline of advancing years. In that, many of his friends have counted Rutherford fortunate, also. But his colleagues, co-workers in the physical sciences, ill-prepared to lose a Rutherford at any time, were doubly unfortunate in the season of his death. He had planned to retire from his position as Director of the Cavendish Laboratory in the summer of 1941, towards the end of his seventieth year, but a great deal remained for him to do in the way of reorganization before that date. His senior staff had been depleted by a long sequence of appointments to professorships: Blackett to Birkbeck College, Chadwick to Liverpool, Ellis to King's College, London, and Oliphant to Birmingham, and it was none too easy for him to replace so many proved men in a short space of years. Then, in the matter of buildings and equipment, also, the laboratory was in the middle of the largest single upheaval in its history.

We have already mentioned Rutherford's determination that the new attack on the problems of the nucleus should not be held up, in Cambridge, by any avoidable lack of material resources; this great upheaval in the laboratory—which, undoubtedly, he did not relish for its own sake—was the direct outcome of that determination. He often said that he had hoped to leave the questions of rebuilding and reorganization to his successor, for they required the energy of youth to carry them through to completion, but events decreed otherwise; his " boys " required larger buildings and new equipment, if their contribution to research in nuclear physics was to keep abreast of the times, and Rutherford saw to it that they obtained them. As he had done fifteen years previously, he again drew up a detailed statement of " The requirements of the Cavendish Laboratory for the future development of its work ". Endowment funds were needed for furnishing skilled technical assistance, for increasing the workshop staff, and for the purchase of special apparatus which was too costly to be bought out of the normal university grant. In addition, new buildings were required: " . . . amongst the important physical laboratories of the world the Cavendish must rank almost lowest in its building amenities ", Rutherford wrote. In the projected buildings the research of the department might be accommodated—with an increase in its range and efficiency—and teaching and administration benefit, also, from greater concentration in the older portions of the laboratory. A total of about £250,000 was the estimated amount of money involved. Mr. Baldwin was then Prime Minister, as well as Chancellor of the university, and this scheme was made known to him. On 30th April, 1936, in his capacity as Chancellor, he was able to announce that Sir Herbert Austin had offered the whole amount to the university for the purposes which Rutherford had outlined. It was a splendid benefaction, and it drew immediate applause from all friends of science in the country. Chadwick wrote to his former chief,[1]

[1] 4th May, 1936.

" It was a tremendous surprise to see the good news.
. . . Begging, like swindling, is only respectable on
a big scale."

—and so, perhaps, it is, but Rutherford was left with
the immense task of bringing to fruition the great
schemes which he had formulated. About a year before
he died, the first part of the building was complete;
a separate laboratory had been erected, specially de-
signed for housing the large-scale apparatus for the
production and application of high voltages in studies
of nuclear transmutation. The apparatus itself was
rapidly installed, and, before the year was out, one
complete set was in full operation. Rutherford was
greatly delighted with the preliminary working of this
apparatus, and the prospect for the future, but the joy
of possession, and its responsibilities, and the task of
supervising the carrying out of the major part of the
schemes of reorganization and construction, passed to
his successor, through the operation of an inexorable
fate. Truly, his colleagues were doubly unfortunate in
the season of his death.

In bringing to its conclusion this appreciation of the
life and achievement of one of the greatest experimental
physicists whom the world has known, a sense of in-
adequacy is uppermost in the mind of the writer. So
much has been omitted of Rutherford's scientific achievement, so many of his public services have been mentioned
only by implication, so little of his part in the ordinary
affairs of life has even been hinted at, that the portrait
must necessarily be incomplete. This is the more regret-
table as Rutherford treasured his contacts with his
fellows more completely, perhaps, than most great
men of science have ever done. He was the antithesis

of the " professor ", as commonly conceived. " With all my other duties I am kept very fully occupied," he wrote to Arthur Smithells when he was deluged with the work of reconstruction which has just been described,[1] " . . . but I will let you know if there is a chance for a mouthful of human speech." He might have written similarly to scores of other correspondents at almost any period of his busy life.

There is one class of correspondent, which is not usually referred to in the biographies of great men, which deserves mention at this stage. All famous men, all well-known scientists in particular, perhaps, are worried by these correspondents from time to time. They are plagued with long letters from uneducated or misguided persons who imagine that they have made some startling discovery or that they have established some flaw in commonly-accepted arguments, which they do not understand. Rutherford almost always acknowledged their letters briefly but kindly; occasionally he put himself to considerable trouble to do his best to satisfy these people that he was not treating them as beneath consideration. He humbled rather than exalted himself in all his replies:

" As I told you, I read your views with interest and I thought them well presented, but I, even more than yourself, have only an amateur knowledge of this very big and intricate problem,"

he wrote [2] when an unemployed New Zealand engineer sent him a long account of his views regarding a possible cure for all deficiency diseases—and, five days later, as it happened, he attempted to comfort one of the long

[1] 14th October, 1936.   [2] 8th May, 1936.

line of disappointed persons who have believed in the possibility of perpetual motion,[1]

> " In my position I am accustomed to receive a large number of letters from cranks of every kind, but I may say that your letter is a notable exception, for it is obviously the inquiry of a reasonable man who knows what he is talking about, but has fallen into an error which is not uncommon. I trust that this will encourage rather than discourage you in trying to understand problems of heat. . . . You may be interested to know that less than 100 years ago, scientific men as a whole failed completely to interpret the type of problem to which you have given attention."

That Rutherford was moved to write two such letters of reply in the course of a single week provides some idea of the amount of his time which he must have given towards reasoning with the uninformed in their folly.

The complete monopoly of folly, however, is not with the uninformed, alone, and Rutherford was equally concerned to remove all traces of it when he found it amongst his students or his colleagues. Here is good advice which he addressed to an old acquaintance who sent, for his criticism, a research student's paper, before publication:

> " I thought that it was a little over enthusiastic and also a little inclined to point out the mote in the other fellow's eye. It is my experience that it is very undesirable for workers in the same field and to some

[1] 13th May, 1936.

extent closely connected to get into too pugnacious habits. I generally preach to my youngsters on the dangers of this attitude which is characteristic of the young. It is not necessary after scalping a victim to wave the scalp in the air and utter a war whoop!"

Rutherford, the peacemaker—it is not perhaps the first epithet which springs to mind, but when the rival claims of scientists were in question he frequently acted the part of self-appointed mediator. "It is thus, I think, of some international importance," he once wrote to the Assistant Secretary of the Royal Society,[1] "that Professor —— should be given an opportunity to express his views shortly in a journal of such wide publicity as that of the *Proceedings of the Royal Society*. I should like to mention that some of the expressions in the original paper have been considerably watered down to preserve peace between the nations!" In this passage, "peace between the nations" is obviously extravagant phrasing, but there was one large inter-national problem towards the solution of which Ruther-ford lent the whole weight of his example, in unremitting service. For four years he was chairman of the Society for the Protection of Science and Learning, and he took a leading and very active part in the attempt to find timely help for the many scholars whom the course of events in Europe had thrown upon the charity of their fellows in foreign lands. To one of these exiles, on 7th October, 1937, he wrote, as to a personal friend,

"I have just returned from a good holiday in the country, and I am leaving for India at the end of November to preside over a joint conference of the

[1] 19th March, 1935.

British Association and the Indian Science Congress at Calcutta. I have not been to India before, and I shall be glad of the opportunity of seeing something of that country."

It was not to be. Ernest Rutherford, we know, died less than a fortnight after that letter had been written.

Index

Note: Quotations are indicated by page numbers printed in italics.